ABOUT...

SUSAN STOKES

Susan Stokes has been a nutrition counselor with the Heart Association for two years. She has worked with the Weber County Extension Service Advisory Council for 4 years and currently is assisting in redesigning life-styles for the patients in the cardiac rehabilitation program at local hospitals. She has experimented with recipes all of her adult life, coming from a home where her mother is an extraordinary cook in her own rights. She has tested all of the Family Favorite recipes on her own family of 10 and many willing friends to refine the quality and flavor for your enjoyment.

Her educational background has always been centered in the nutrition field and along with the book learning her practical experience brings her into the ranks of expert.

Her efforts to educate herself have lead to this tremendous collection of recipes that have been healthified. She has authored three cook books prior to joining efforts with Thornock International Productions, Inc. to bring you this most recent compilation as an author for the fourth time.

THORNOCK INTERNATIONAL PRODUCTIONS, INC.

Van and Chris Thornock, brother and sister, have spent the past five years designing, co-authoring and producing products in the field of health and nutrition. Their main emphasis has been in developing and producing the EAT & Be Lean program.

This book represents an expanded effort by Van and Chris to further provide you and your family the variety you desire to EAT & Be Lean while enjoying the taste of fine family tested recipes. Only the most favorite recipes have been compiled and are designed to move you towards a healthier cooking style. Enjoy!

O. VAN THORNOCK

Vans business background in managing mortgage lending offices for over 17 years formed the business foundation for Thornock International Productions, Inc. He is the chief executive officer of the company. Van has a variety of talents that he has developed and used to help bring this publication together. He has developed and produced numerous video and audio productions and is the photographer of the foods displayed in the *EAT & Be Lean Favorite Family Recipes* book.

CHRISCILLA M. THORNOCK

Chris received her undergraduate degree in communications design, coaching and teaching. She worked as head women's athletic trainer for Weber State University for five years designing health, fitness and rehabilitation programs for both the men's and women's athletic teams. Her masters degree was in Professional Leadership from Brigham Young University with a third degree from Art Center College of Design in Industrial Design. She has owned her own technical graphics design business and currently writes and designs products for Thornock International Productions, Inc. Chris co-authored the original EAT & Be Lean student manual that has sold over 40,000 copies. She is the technical graphics layout designer and illustrator of the *EAT &*

ACKNOWLEDGMENTS

It is with gratitude and appreciation that we acknowledge the efforts and dedication of the many people who have helped bring a production of this magnitude to fruition. Countless hours and cooperation are essential and have been freely contributed by all to ensure its completion.

A special thanks to our spouses and children in the Stokes, Thornock and Humpherys families for their patience and assistance and long suffering.

Thanks to Susan's mother, Lois Hobbs for teaching her, inspiring her, and instilling a curiosity about and a love for cooking.

Our love and thanks to Wayne and EuVola Thornock for their endless contributions towards our success.

Thorelle Abbott has rendered her expertise and been very dedicated in preparing shopping lists and keeping the office running in our absence.

Gloria Woodward, Vicki Robison, Heidi Neumarker and Jan Greenwell have generously provided us with additional recipes and we gratefully acknowledge the time they have spent.

EAT & Be Lean™ BASIC NUTRITION

INTRODUCTION

Understanding a few basic principles about health and nutrition will be of great benefit to you and your family in conjunction with the recipes and menu plans presented in this cookbook. Whether you are the bread winner or the bread maker of your household it is important to be educated about the affects different types of foods, exercise, artificial sweeteners, drugs and thoughts have on your body. Stating it simply, you are what you eat.

With these things in mind, we will introduce you to the truth about the four food groups. The dairy association developed the basic four food groups many years ago to ensure the increased demand for dairy products. The elementary schools received free charts to be hung up in the class room for constant review. The groups that they taught are the Vegetable Group, Fruit Group, Meat Group and Dairy Group.

In actuality, there are four food groups, but dairy is included with the meat group and grains are rightfully introduced as their own group. The true four food groups are vegetables, grains, fruits and proteins. Water is another important part of the group and should be present at every meal and between meals.

Eating should be a pleasure? If it is not a pleasure to you, something is not correct in your understanding of food, what it does and why you need large amounts of food to maximize your body's potential.

It is important to eat often and understand the effect of what you are eating, to enable your metabolism to increase. Eating frequently and to complete satisfaction will provide your muscles with the high caloric requirements for leaner, stronger muscle tissue. By skipping meals, your metabolism is slowed dramatically, slowing your calorie burning and increasing your fat storage. That is the reason we provide you with a lot of food both during the meals as well as the snacks between meals in our menu plan section. If fat loss is your goal, it's valuable to know that people who eat six times a day tend to lose nearly twice as fast as those who eat three times a day.

If eating often to complete satisfaction can make you lean, it only stands to reason that diets do not work. Dieting increases the tendency for fat storage and obesity. It is true that one person in 200 will be able to stay starved skinny, but their body begins to cannibalize itself to maintain life. Under this starvation condition, good health (both mental and physical) is difficult to maintain. Rapid aging with dieters and the incidence of premature death increases is dramatic.

As you begin to healthify your body by eating often and to complete satisfaction, you will find that the obsessions for excess fats and sweets will diminish. Those cravings will be replaced with a natural desire for nutritious foods. As you learn to balance your meals with water, vegies, grains, fruits and proteins, fat loss and optimum health will follow.

Research clearly indicates that eating excess fat is what makes you fat. The American diet typically consists of 40%-50% fat during an average day of eating. It is no wonder why Americans are literally the most out of shape group of people in the world today. If you eat 50% fat, you'll become 50% fat. If you eat 15% to 20% fat, you will be within the range of maximum health and lean-ness.

There are 10 main negative stressors that cause ill health and obesity that are discussed in detail in the EAT & Be Lean Student Manual, but for the sake of brevity and getting on with testing the recipes that follow, the ten main negative stressors are:

1. dieting
2. no exercise or excess exercise
3. negative thinking
4. alcohol and certain drugs
5. caffeine (coffee/tea)
6. excess fat
7. artificial sweeteners
8. refined carbohydrates (causing excess insulin)
9. excess protein
10. allergies and/or gastro intestinal distress

These are the contributing factors to poor health and increasing obesity no matter what the age, sex, height or hereditary background. The more of these stressful behaviors you are able to eliminate from your life-style, the healthier your body will become.

Since artificial sweeteners have been found to possibly cause fat gain more rapidly than regular sugar, you will not find any recipes in this book that contain such things as Equal (Nutrasweet), Saccharin, Sweet and Low, etc.. Research indicates that there can be considerable damage to the body and brain through the use of artificial sweeteners; even death has been attributed to their use. If there were such a thing as a forbidden food, this would be the one; but then, artificial sweeteners cannot be considered real food.

No foods are really forbidden. Rather than forbidding all deserts (which will surely cause mental cravings anyway), you need to know that the sugars (refined carbohydrates) are absorbed into the blood stream at a slower rate and are more easily eliminated from the body when consumed *immediately after* eating to complete satisfaction on the more complex foods. The body has an amazing ability to compensate for harmful substances for a period of time before sustaining permanent damage. You will find that the more fats and sweet choices you make, the more sluggish and lousy you will feel. Fats and sweets are not lasting, healthful, energy choices. You can eat that dessert, but you will surely feel the consequences for a period of time. People who choose to reduce and even eliminate them from their daily eating routines find they can no longer tolerate them in large amounts if any. There are many desserts in this book to choose from. Some have been completely healthified and others move down in the "health grading". We realize there is a transitional period as you healthify your body and there will be occasions with guests and parties where you need to provide a dessert that meets everyone's minimum requirements for sweetness. We have still reduced the fat, blended whole grains into the recipes and tried to remove as many sugars as possible. **Fructose** is assimilated into the body like a **complex carbohydrate** rather than a simple sugar. For this reason we have replaced the refined carbohydrates (ie. white sugar, honey, molasses, brown sugar) as much as possible with fructose. Some desserts are still unhealthifyable. Use your own discretion and be moderate with the use of any desserts.

As you begin to healthify your body by eliminating the negative stressors we have presented to you, you will notice a wonderful sense of well-being and find that your appetite will increase. It increases naturally to ensure that you provide the proper amount of calories now necessary for your increased metabolism.

One of the most important things you can learn to do is to relax, educate yourself about foods and let the magic begin. Practice simple positive affirmations that help you feel good about who you are today and what you will be tomorrow. Chapter five in the EAT & Be Lean Student Manual will help you understand more fully how easy it is to program yourself mentally for physical success.

For more detailed information on health and nutrition for the entire family, you can purchase the EAT & Be Lean™ Student Manual in your local bookstore, or order it by phone or mail using the following information:

EAT & Be Lean
P.O. Box 1132
Clearfield, UT 84015
801-776-1176

Our philosophy is, "If it doesn't taste good...why eat it?" Your philosophy can and should be the same. Now, enjoy the low-fat family favorites that are provided for your pleasure in the following pages.

READ THE LABEL

DO NOT BE FOOLED...

1. Don't be fooled by labels that say, "Low Fat", "Lite", "No Cholesterol", "95% Fat Free", etc.
2. Look for the amount of fat per serving - usually listed in grams of fat.
3. What kind of fat has been used. Read the list of ingredients.
4. Serving size - many times high fat items will list a much smaller than usual serving size. Who really eats 1/2 of a candy bar, 1/4 cup of granola, or 1/2 cup of ice cream?
5. Does food require any additions before eating - such as pudding mixes, cake mixes, macaroni and cheese, etc.
6. Watch out for any label that says "vegetable oils", or "assorted palm, coconut or other oils." If the label does not specify which oil is being used, suspect the worst.

If the grams of fat information is not on the label, pay particular attention to the ingredient list. Ingredients are listed in descending order. Where is the fat in that order? Is it among the first three or four ingredients, or among the last few? Higher in the list means more of it. Is fat listed more than once - such as vegetable oil in one place, cream in another? Many times a manufacturer will list an ingredient such as fat or sugar several different places (using different names) to avoid having to list it first.

Use a reference publication for food without labels, such as meat, fish, poultry, etc. It will give you information on all of the nutrients in the food, including grams of fat.

RECIPE HEALTHIFICATION

DELICIOUS AND HEALTHY...

You can prepare food that is both delicious and good for you!

1. Learn to balance higher fat foods with low or no-fat foods to result in a meal in which 20% or less of the calories come from fat.

2. Invest in some non-stick cookware. It will become indispensable. Use for "sauteing" and "frying".

3. Should the ingredient be eliminated, reduced, or should a substitute be used?

4. Is there a better cooking method?

5. How often do you eat the food? It is more important to cut down on the fatty foods you eat daily, than it is to cut out a food you eat only occasionally.

6.   How much of the food do you eat? Sometimes decreasing the quantity is more satisfying than decreasing the quality. If you really like standard pie crust for instance, maybe you would be better off making a one crust pie with a low fat filling, or just eating a smaller piece. On the other hand, some people find going without a favorite high fat food easier than having just a little.

7.   Use fats and oils sparingly. You can almost always cut way back on the fat or oil in a recipe and sometimes eliminate them altogether without changing the taste.

8.   Baked goods: Try reducing fat by 1/3 to 1/2. If this is successful, try reducing even more. This works very well in quick breads, muffins, cookies, and "heavier" cakes (like applesauce cake.) Replace fat or oil with another ingredient such as mashed banana, applesauce, shredded carrot, zucchini, or apple, orange juice, apple juice, pineapple juice, buttermilk or yogurt.

9.   When you reduce the fat by about 1/3, sugar can also be reduced by about 1/4.

10.   Entrees: Cut way back or eliminate added fat. Use non-stick cookware. Use vegetable oil spray. Use smaller amounts of the leanest meats, 2 to 3 ounces per person, (3 oz. of meat is about the size of a deck of cards) and remove all visible fat.

11.   Watch the amount of cheese you used. Use a small amount of highly flavored cheese such as extra sharp cheddar or parmesan. You will get wonderful flavor using much less cheese.

12.   Eliminate fatty sauces and gravies or make your own low-fat substitutions. This can be easily done by using a fat free broth, thickening it with corn starch, Wondra flour or, better yet, whole wheat flour. Simply season to taste.

13.   Add more grains and vegetables to your meals.

14.   Choose low or no fat dairy products.

15.   Watch out for fat in prepared foods that you want to use along with your own recipes.

For more ideas on healthifying your recipes, refer to the EAT & Be Lean manual in the healthification section.

NOTE: Choose wisely when eating out and don't be upset over an occasional splurge. Remember, the body is very forgiving when you provide it with the vitamins and nutrients it needs.

FOOD SUBSTITUTIONS

HEALTHY CREATIVE SUBSTITUTIONS REPLACE UNHEALTHY FOODS...

USE THIS...	INSTEAD OF ...
Skim milk	Whole milk
Evaporated skim milk	Cream or whipping cream
Plain nonfat yogurt or lite sour cream	Sour Cream
Fat free or low-fat cottage cheese	Cream cheese or sour cream
Plain nonfat yogurt, drained or Fat free cream cheese	Cream cheese
Low-fat and fat free cheeses	High-fat cheeses
Sorbet, non fat frozen yogurt, sherbet, fat free frozen desserts	Ice Cream
Fat free or reduced calorie mayonnaise, mustard, ketchup	Regular mayonnaise
Kraft Fat Free Peppercorn Ranch Salad Dressing	Mayonnaise for tuna and chicken sandwiches
No or low-fat dressings	Regular Salad dressings
Fish - poached, baked, broiled, steamed	Fish - breaded or fried
Water packed tuna	Oil packed tuna
Poultry without skin and fat	Poultry with skin
Lean well trimmed beef - (top round, eye-of-round, top sirloin) or pork - tenderloin	Regular marbled cuts of beef
Moderate portions of meat	Large portions of meat
Low-fat sauces and marinades	High-fat sauces and marinades
Healthy Request low-fat creamed soups	Canned cream soups
Low-fat ramen	Regular Ramen
Bouillon, herbs, broth, juices	High-fat gravy and sauce
Low-fat cooking methods (broil, bake, boil, poach, steam)	High-fat cooking methods (frying, cooking in own fat)
Dry beans and peas	Meat
Meatless sauces	Sauces with meat
Fat free or low-fat spaghetti sauce	Regular jar spaghetti sauce
Steamed vegies with herbs spices, lemon juice, low-fat sauces	Veggies with butter, cheese sauce, fried vegies
Water chestnuts	Nuts in Veggie casseroles
Unbuttered popcorn (air pop)	Buttered popcorn, chips, fries
Micro-baked "chips" or "fries"	Potato chips, french fries
Homemade tortilla chips, pita crisps Wonton chips	Tortilla chips, snack crackers
Pretzels	Chips, snack crackers, nuts
Whole grain bread, bagel, muffin	Doughnuts, pastries
Bread sticks, low-fat snack crackers	High-fat snack crackers

USE THIS...	INSTEAD OF ...
Lower fat cookies: Gingersnaps, fig bars, graham crackers, animal crackers	High-fat cookies
Angel food cake	High-fat cakes
Fresh fruit	High-fat desserts
Puddings made with skim milk	Puddings made with whole milk
Reduced fat cake and brownie mixes	Cake and brownie mix
All fruit jelly, jam, honey on toast	Butter or margarine on toast
Yogurt-cheese or fat free cream bagel cheese on toast or bagel	Cream cheese on toast or

MEATLESS DINNERS AND LUNCHES: Learn to have some.

Vegetable soups with beans, grains and/or pasta in them make a wonderful, filling meal.

Spaghetti with meatless sauce, orientals style cooking (lots of vegetables and a small amount of meat) are a good choice.

SNACKS:

Plan your snacks. If you are used to having snacks you are already in moving in the right direction. In planning your snacks, remember that vegetables, being the most complex of the complex carbohydrates, should be your first choice. Work down in the complexity by choosing grain snacks second, fruit snacks third and lastly proteins. Avoid sweet snacks, fat snacks and those made with refined carbohydrates such as "enriched" or white breads, rolls or muffins. Snacking between meals on complex carbohydrates will increase your fat burning metabolism and increase the bodies efficiency.

GROUND BEEF GOES LEAN

Here are some tips for cooking lean ground beef.

■ Use a low heat setting when browning to avoid hard, crusty surfaces, and don't over cook.

■ When making loaves, patties, or meatballs, don't over fix; mixtures will have a firm compact texture.

■ Add liquids sparingly when making mixtures to avoid a soft texture that may not hold together well.

■ How lean is lean? Ground beef is sold from 73% to 95% lean by weight. But when you take a look at the total grams of fat the ground beef contains after it's cooked, you get a better picture of the "big fat" difference.

Ground beef sold as	Contains grams of total fat*
73% lean	17.9 grams
80% lean	15.2 grams
85% lean	12.2 grams
90% lean	9.1 grams
95% lean	4.9 grams
*Per 3-ounce cooked serving (broiled, medium)	

Rebecca J. Pate, Director of the Cooking Light *Test Kitchens.*

Cooking Light Magazine, pg. 158

1st CHOICE INGREDIENTS

RECOMMENDED INGREDIENTS FOR *EAT & Be Lean FAMILY FAVORITE* **RECIPES...**
If a menu or recipe calls for an ingredient your family does not care for, substitute!

Milk is skim, nonfat powdered or skim evaporated (1 FG rather than 20 per cup like regular evaporated milk).

Buttermilk can be dry or fluid. Saco brand dry can be mixed in with the dry ingredients, add water for liquid. Be sure to read labels on fluid buttermilk. There are differences in fat between brands.

Dream Whip does have Palm Kernel oil, but is still a good choice in many recipes. Use it sparingly. Whipping skim evaporated milk, or powdered milk does not give satisfactory results in most cases. Dream Whip, made with skim milk, has a lower amount of fat than cream or other substitutes for cream. Remember, in most recipes, you are eating a couple of tablespoons, not a cup. Freeze in serving size dollops.

Sour cream is light, 1 gram of fat per tablespoon.

Ricotta is nonfat.

Low-fat Mozzarella cheese has 2 grams of fat per ounce or less.

Low-fat Cheddar and Swiss cheeses have 5 grams fat per ounce or less.

Fat free singles has 0 grams of fat per slice

Parmesan cheese is fresh instead of pre-grated canned.

Dannon nonfat yogurt, drained, for yogurt cheese. If a richer texture is desired, use Dannon low-fat yogurt.

Vegetables and fruits are fresh or frozen, unless specified.

Salad dressings (homemade or purchase) are no or very low-fat.

Poultry has skin and fat removed before cooking.

Broth for soup, sauce, or gravy is always de-fatted before use.

Egg whites are from large eggs. Two large egg whites (eliminating the fat in the yolk) equals 1 whole egg. Use the same ration if cholesterol is a problem and further reductions need to be made.

Egg substitutes are more expensive but less fat. These products are basically egg whites with some fat and other ingredients taking the place of the yolk.

Crackers, breads, and rolls (purchased or homemade) should be whole grain, and very low or no fat varieties.

Brown rice, bulgur, and **couscous** in the bulk section or import aisle at the supermarket, or check Middle East markets, and Health Food stores.

Egg roll wrappers and **Wonton wrappers** are always in a refrigerated case - usually by the produce department.

Frozen yogurts or desserts (ice milk substitute) should be non-fat. "Fat substitutes" such as "Simpless" should be avoided.

FAVORITE
FAMILY
RECIPES

**Delicious, Transitional
Recipes Towards Healthier
Low-fat, Low-sugar Cooking**

Published by Thornock International Productions, Inc.

FAVORITE FAMILY RECIPES

Delicious, Transitional Recipes Towards Healthier Low-fat, Low-sugar Cooking

Copyright © 1992 by
THORNOCK INTERNATIONAL
PRODUCTIONS, INC.

First Printing, November 1992

ISBN # 0-9629060-3-4

Printed in the United States of America

A SPECIAL NOTE
To EAT & Be Lean GRADUATES and NEWCOMERS

You will notice that many of the recipes in this book use half whole wheat flour and half enriched white flour. These recipes are designed as transitional recipes to help you and your family naturally move towards healthier food choices by first *reducing* the fat and sugar. Gradually the refined carbohydrates (white flour and sugar) should be reduced further and eventually eliminated from the recipes. The ideal ingredients to cook with are fresh 100% stone ground whole grain flour instead of white flour, and honey, fruit juice concentrate, or fructose instead of sugar. This, however, can take a little time for a families tastes to adjust to.

For those of you who have already made the transition from refined carbohydrates to complex carbohydrates, the recipes will only require the smallest amount of alteration to become completely healthified.

CONTENTS

SNACKS & APPETIZERS

BEVERAGES

SOUPS & SAUCES

BREADS

MENU PLANS

BREAKFAST

INGREDIENT INDEX

DESSERTS

RECIPE INDEX

DIPS, DRESSINGS

PRODUCTS

MAIN DISHES

MISCELLANEOUS

SALADS

SIDE DISHES

"The chief cause of failure and unhappiness is trading what we want most for what we want at the moment."

Author Unknown

Breads and Grains

Pumpkin Bread Loaf - page 10 Cranberry Bread Loaf - 8
Banana Bread Loaf - 7

Cranberry Bread, Banana Bread

Breakfast Suggestions

Good Morning Wheat Cereal - page 15
Applesauce Bran Muffins - 6

Applesauce Carrot-Oat Muffin - page 6
Rice Pudding In An Instant - page 48
Breakfast Compote - page 14

Granola and Yogurt Parfait - page 15
Fruit Filled Bran Muffins - page 9

MENU IDEA: Whole Grain Bagel with
Fat Free Cream Cheese or YOGURT CHEESE^ page 107
and All Fruit Jam, Fresh Fruit

**Individual Breakfast Cups - page 16, 82
and Fresh Fruit**

Fillo Tarts (on cover) - page 33

**Turkey Salad With A Twist - page 115
and Baked Yam**

Sticky Chicken - page 94 and a Tossed Salad

Simply Wonderful Orange Roughy - page 89
Spinach Citrus Salad - page 115
Sweet and Sour Dressing - page 61

**Tex-Mex Rice - page 125, Fillo Wrapped Chimichangas - page 78,
Warm Calico Salad - page 116**

Oven Fries - page 123, Baked Chicken Nuggets - page 65

Stacee's Gone All Afternoon Stew - 94

Green Tomato Ratatouille - page 80

Taco Salad
Crispy Dessert Shell - page 31
Corn Tortilla Chips - page 128

Taco Salad and Corn Chips - pages 31 and 128

Rainbow Salad - page 112, Sweet and Sour Dressing - page 61

Jicama-Carrot Slaw In Pepper Rings- page 113

Shrimp Dip - page 60, Suggestions For Dippers - page 56

**Seafood Party Appetizer - page 132, 12:00 - 3:00 Bagel Crisps - page 128,
3:00 - 6:00 Ry-Krisps, 6:00 - 8:00 Pita Crisps - page 131,
8:00 - 10:00 Nabisco Snack-Wel Crackers, 10:00 - 12:00 Ry Krisp Wheat Cracker**

LAST NOTES

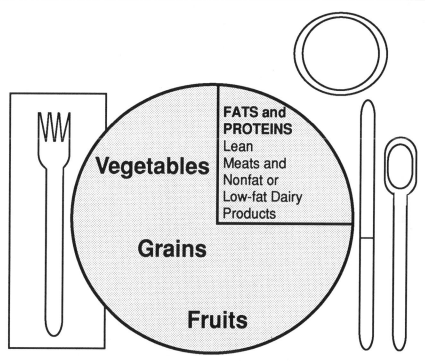

65 - 80% of the food on your plate should be in the form of complex carbohydrates such as vegetables, grains and fruits. Proteins should be in the range of 10 - 15% and fats in the range of 15 - 20%.

EXAMPLE:

W   12 oz.
V   1 cup mushrooms, 1 cup green peas, tossed salad with nonfat dressing
G   2 cups brown rice pilaf
F   1 cup fruit cocktail
P   6 oz. halibut steak

REMEMBER:

If the recipe makes 6 servings and you eat 1/3 of it by yourself, your counts will be different than those given at the top of the recipe.

EAT & Be Lean Favorite Family Recipes have been analyzed using the software program, "The Better Diet Analyzer". When nutritive information was not in the program, the package information was used or "The Complete Book of Food Counts" by Corinne Netzer. Complete accuracy is difficult because of the differences in ingredients.

BEVERAGES

APRICOT DELIGHT
By Susan Stokes

Serves 2   **Serving Size = 1/2 Cup**   **213 Calories**   **0 Fat Grams**

Put into blender container:

1 cup	non-fat yogurt
1 cup	**thick** apricot nectar
1 large	**ripe** banana
2 Tbl.	frozen orange or pineapple juice concentrate
5 or 6	ice cubes

Blend on high speed until thick and creamy. When I am rushed in the morning, I toss 1/3 cup oats in with the rest of the ingredients. Blend as usual. Tihs makes a quick breakfast in a glass.

CHRISTMAS PUNCH
By Susan Stokes

Serves 30   **Serving Size = 2/3 Cup**   **62 Calories**   **0 Fat Grams**

12 oz. can	frozen orange juice concentrate, prepared as directed
6 cups	cranberry juice cocktail
1 quart	gingerale, chilled

Stir juices together and chill. Add gingerale just before serving. Yields about 30 punch cups.

DOUBLE PINEAPPLE PUNCH
By Susan Stokes

Serves 30   **Serving Size = 2/3 Cup**   **89 Calories**   **Fat Grams = t**

2 cans	lite pears, chilled (29 oz.)	4 cups	Lemon-Lime Soda (1/2 of a 2 liter bottle), chilled
12 oz. can	lemonade, thawed		
3 cups	pineapple juice, chilled	1 quart	pineapple sherbet, made into balls
2 cups	cold water		

Drain 1 can of pears. Blend pears with the juice from the un-drained can. Pour pear puree, lemonade concentrate, pineapple juice, and water into a chilled punch bowl; stir to blend. Add lemon-lime soda, stir very briefly. Add sherbet and serve in punch cups.

NOTES

HOT SPICED PUNCH
By Susan Stokes

Serves 30   **Serving Size = 1 cup**   **117 Calories**   **0 Fat Grams**

1 cups	honey
4 cups	hot water
1 tsp.	whole cloves
10 whole	allspice berries
4 sticks	cinnamon
1/3 cup	red hot cinnamon candies

Tie cloves and allspice berries in a piece of cheesecloth. Put all ingredients in a large stainless steel or enamel pan, bring to a boil. Turn heat down and simmer for 5 minutes. Remove from heat and let stand several hours or overnight. Remove spice bag and cinnamon sticks.

Add:

6 oz. can	frozen orange juice concentrate
2 cans	frozen lemonade concentrate (small)
2 quarts	apple cider or apple juice
48 oz.	cranberry juice
2 - 3 qts.	water (to taste)

Reheat and serve -- DO NOT BOIL after you add juices.

LAST MINUTE HOLIDAY PUNCH
By Susan Stokes

Serves 1   **Serving Size = 1/3 Cup**   **138 Calories**   **Fat Grams = t**

Place 1 scoop orange sherbet in each glass. Fill with chilled cranberry juice.

NON-ALCOHOLIC BUBBLY
By Susan Stokes

Reconstitute frozen apple juice concentrate with sparkling water. Cranberry juice concentrate is very nice too! Look for the no-sugar choices.

NOTES

STRAWBERRY BANANA BLENDER BREAKFAST DRINK
By Susan Stokes

Serves 2   **Serving Size = 1 1/2 Cup**   **238 Calories**   **Fat Grams = t**

Put into blender container:

2 cups	cold skim milk
1 1/2 cups	individually frozen strawberries
1 large	banana (ripe)
2 Tbl.	orange or pineapple juice concentrate
1 Tbl.	fructose

Blend on high speed until smooth and creamy.

WARM AND SPICY TOMATO JUICE
By Susan Stokes

Serves 8   **Serving Size = 1 Cup**   **641 Calories**   **0 Fat Grams**

8 cups	tomato juice	1 tsp.	fructose
1/3 cup	fresh lemon juice	1/4 tsp.	garlic powder
1-3/4 tsp.	Worcestershire sauce	1/8 tsp.	onion powder
1/2 tsp.	hot pepper sauce		

Combine all ingredients. Heat on stove or in microwave until hot, stirring occasionally. Pour into mugs. Garnish with a twist of lemon.

NOTES

BREADS

APPLE CARROT- OAT MUFFINS
By Susan Stokes

Makes 12	Serving Size = 1 Piece	116 Calories	1.5 Fat Grams

These are good hot or cold. Leftovers make a terrific snack.

1/2 cup	raisins covered with 1/2 cup warm apple juice	2	egg whites
		1 Tbl.	honey
1 cup	w.w. flour	1/3 cup	fructose
3/4 cup	quick rolled oats	1 Tbl.	margarine, melted
1 tsp.	baking soda	1/4 tsp.	vanilla
1/2 tsp.	salt	1/8 tsp.	lemon extract
1 tsp.	cinnamon	1 cup	applesauce
1/4 tsp.	nutmeg	3/4 cup	grated carrot

Preheat oven to 400 degrees. Line twelve muffin cups with aluminum liners. Mix all of the dry ingredients in a large bowl. Combine egg whites, fructose, honey, margarine, vanilla, and lemon extract in a small bowl, whisk together, stir in applesauce and grated carrot. Add this mixture and the raisins with their liquid to the dry ingredients. Stir only until blended. Fill each muffin cup 3/4 full. Bake 18 minutes.

APPLESAUCE - BRAN MUFFINS
By Susan Stokes

Makes 12	Serving Size = 1 muffin	100 Calories	1.5 Fat Grams

1 1/2 cups	All Bran Cereal	1/3 cup	all purpose flour
3/4 cup	skim milk	2/3 cup	whole wheat flour
2	egg white, slightly beaten	2 tsp.	baking powder
1/2 cup	applesauce	1/2 tsp.	baking soda
1 Tbl.	Canola oil (Cold pressed)	1/4 tsp.	salt
3 T	honey		

Preheat oven to 400 degrees. Whisk cereal, milk, egg whites, applesauce and oil and honey. In a large bowl, combine flour, baking powder, baking powder, baking soda and salt, and sugar. Pour in liquid mixture; stir until just blended. Line a muffin tin with baking cups (aluminum liners work great!). Fill each cup 3/4 full. Bake for 15 minutes, or until nicely browned. "I like to stir 1/2 cup raisins or other dried chopped fruit into the batter ."

NOTES

BANANA BREAD
By Susan Stokes

Makes 3 loaves (16 slices per loaf)   **Serving Size = 1 Slice**   **86 Calories**   **2 Fat Grams**

BREADS

Very nice flavored bread. Makes 3 loaves.

6 ripe	bananas	2 tsp.	baking powder
1/4 cup	honey	2 1/2 cups	flour (whole wheat)
1 1/4 cups	fructose	1 1/2 cup	all purpose flour
1/4 cup	honey	1 tsp.	salt
3 Tbl.	Canola oil (cold pressed)	1/2 cup	walnuts or pecans, finely
1/3 cup	applesauce or plain non-fat yogurt		chopped (measure before
1 tsp.	vanilla		chopping) OR 1/3 cup
1	egg plus 4 egg whites		poppy seeds
2 Tbl.	warm water	2 tsp.	baking soda dissolved in

Preheat oven to 350 degrees. Grease and flour the bottom of 3 (8 1/2 x 4 1/2 x 2 1/2 inch) pans, or spray with Bakers Joy. Mash bananas, add fructose and honey. Let stand 15 minutes. Add oil, applesauce, vanilla, and slightly beaten egg and whites. Stir to mix. Sift or stir together the flour, baking powder and salt ; add to banana mixture along with nuts and dissolved baking soda. Stir only until well mixed, do not over mix. Divide evenly into prepared pans, bake for 45 to 60 minutes or until a toothpick comes out clean. Cool 10 minutes on wire rack, remove from pans and cool completely before wrapping. Freezes well.

Made with poppy seeds and no nut: 16 FG per loaf - 1 FG per slice

BUTTERMILK CORNBREAD
By Gloria Woodward

Serves 16   **Serving Size = 2" x 2"**   **55 Calories**   **2 Fat Gram**

3	egg whites	1/2 tsp.	soda
2 Tbl.	honey	1/2 tsp.	salt
1 cup	buttermilk	2 Tbl.	melted margerine
1 cup	soft white wheat flour	2 tsp.	baking powder
2/3 cup	freshly ground corn flour		

Sift or stir all dry ingredients together. Whisk egg whites until frothy, add honey, margarine and buttermilk. Whisk to combine. Pour liquids into dry ingredients. Stir briefly, just enough to evenly moisten. Immediately pour into 8 x 8 inch pan which has been greased and gloured. Bake 20 minutes at 400 degrees. Serve warm.

NOTES

CRACKED WHEAT BREAD
By Gloria Woodward

Soak raw, cracked wheat a few hours or over night by covering with water. It will expand, soften, and absorb the water. Drain well and add to your bread the last 3 or 4 minutes of kneading.

CRANBERRY BREAD
By Susan Stokes

Serves 3 Loaves   **Serving Size = 1 Slice**   **80 Calories**   **2 Fat Grams**
16 Slices Per Loaf

I learned this recipe from 10th grade cooking class. My family has always loved it! The original recipe says to cut each cranberry in 1/2 and then proceed - now I blender Chop! This recipe makes 3 loaves - one to eat and two to share or freeze for later.

4 cups	fresh cranberries, rinsed, sorted, coarsely chopped	2 tsp.	salt
		1 tsp.	baking soda
1/2 cup	walnuts, finely chopped *	1	egg plus 2 egg whites, well beaten**
3 Tbl.	Butter		
2 cups	all purpose flour	2/3 cup	orange juice
2 cups	whole wheat flour	1/2 cup	water or plain nonfat yogurt
1 3/4 cups	fructose	1 Tbl.	orange peel (fresh grated)
3 1/2 tsp.	baking powder		

   *   **Measure** nuts before chopping.
  ** **You** can use all egg whites if desired (4 egg whites)

Melt butter and set aside to cool. Blender chop the cranberries half at a time using lots of cold water; (don't over process - you want these very coarsely chopped) drain in a strainer. Prepare 3 loaf pans, (8 1/2 x 4 1/2 x 2 1/2 inch pans) by greasing and flouring the bottoms only - this prevents a ridge from forming around the top edge of your bread. Preheat oven to 350 degrees. Combine all of the dry ingredients in a large bowl; stir to mix thoroughly. Stir beaten egg and egg whites, juice, water or yogurt, orange peel, and melted margarine together. Add liquids and chopped cranberries to the dry ingredients. Stir only enough to moisten - do not try to make the batter smooth! Divide evenly into prepared pans. Bake for 45 to 60 minutes, or until a toothpick comes out clean and dry. Place pans on wire racks and cool 10 minutes. Run a thin bladed knife or metal spatula around sides; remove from pans. Cool completely, then wrap - first in plastic wrap, second in foil or a plastic bag. Freezes beautifully. (These loaves will not be as high and rounded as other quick breads)

FLOUR TORTILLAS
By Susan Stokes

Serves 16   **Serving Size = 1**   **88 Calories**   **1 Fat Gram**

1 1/2 cups	all purpose flour	1 tsp.	salt
1 1/2 cups	w.w. flour	1 1/2 cups	warm water
1 1/2 tsp.	baking powder	1 Tbl.	vegetable oil

Stir all dry ingredients together. Add water a little at a time until dough is very soft, but not sticky. Add oil, and knead until dough is soft and satiny. Cover and let rest while griddle heats over medium heat. Make dough balls a little larger then a golf ball. Use a heavy rolling pin for easier rolling. Tortilla should be 5 or 6 inches round (don't worry if it is not as round as store bought!) Lay on hot griddle until bubbles come through the top, turn over and cook until done. You roll out more as you cook. Store in a clean cloth in a covered container, or plastic bag.

FRUIT FILLED BRAN MUFFINS
By Susan Stokes

Makes 12   **Serving Size = 1 Muffin**   **123 Calories**   **2 Fat Grams**

Fantastic moist fruit filled muffins. These are easy to make and they freeze beautifully. If you can not find cranberries in the store, and you have failed to put some in your freezer, just use extra apple.

2/3 cup	whole wheat flour**	1/2 cup	raisins
1/3 cup	all purpose flour	1/3 cup	brown sugar, pack firm
1/3 cup	unprocessed bran**	3 Tbl.	honey
1/3 cup	oat bran**	4 tsp.	Canola oil
1 tsp.	baking powder	1 tsp.	vanilla
1/4 tsp.	baking soda	1 med.	Granny Smith or
1/2 tsp.	cinnamon		Jonathan apple, chopped
1/4 tsp.	salt	3/4 cup	fresh or frozen whole
2	egg whites (large)		cranberries
2 Tbl.	plain non-fat yogurt		

Preheat oven to 375 degrees. Prepare a muffin tin by lining each cup with a foil liner. Stir first seven ingredients together in a large bowl. Put egg whites, yogurt, brown sugar, honey, oil, and vanilla into a small bowl; stir until well blended. Pour liquid ingredients into dry ingredients; add apple, cranberries, and raisins. Stir together using as few strokes as possible - just enough to moisten. Divide evenly into lined muffin cups. Bake 25 to 26 minutes.

** If you don't have all of these ingredients, just use 1 cup all whole wheat and 2/3 cup quick cooking oats.

Note: Foil muffin liners may be difficult to find, but they are worth the effort! Low fat muffins will stick to paper liners; foil peels right off. Look for them in the same area as paper liners - ask your store manager to order them if you can't find them.

GARLIC CHEESE TOAST
By Susan Stokes

Serves 4   **Serving Size = 1 Slice**   **102 Calories**   **3 Fat Grams**

Ingredients per serving:

4 thick slices	whole wheat buns or French bread
1 Tbl.	Promise Ultra margarine
1 Tbl.	Wishbone Lite Italian Salad dressing
1 1/4 tsp.	Molly McButter Garlic flavor sprinkles
To taste	Mrs. Dash Garlic & Herb salt free Seasoning
2 Tbl.	freshly grated Parmesan cheese
1/3 cup	grated Frigo Truly Light mazzarella cheese

Stir soft margarine, dressing, garlic sprinkles and parmesan together. Lightly toast bread. Divide spread evenly between the 4 slices. Spread. Sprinkle with mozzarella. Place under broiler for a minute or two, or until cheese melts and bubbles.

NOTES

ICE BOX BRAN MUFFINS
By Susan Stokes

Makes 6 dozen **Serving Size = 1 Muffin** **103 Calories** **2 Fat Grams**

2 cups	Bran Buds	3 1/2 cups	whole wheat flour
2 cups	boiling water	1 1/2 cups	all purpose flour
1/2 cup	Canola oil (cold pressed)	5 tsp.	baking soda
2	cups fructose	1 tsp.	salt
2	eggs plus 4 egg whites	4 cups	All Bran cereal
1 qt.	lowfat buttermilk	15 oz.	raisins

Pour boiling water over the Bran Buds. Let stand until water is absorbed. Whisk the vegetable oil, fructose, eggs, and egg whites together, stir in the buttermilk and the Bran Bud mixture, blend well. Stir flour, soda, and salt together in a large bowl. Pour in the buttermilk combination and the All Bran cereal. Stir only until dry ingredients are moist, quickly stir in raisins.

This recipe will store in the refrigerator 5 to 6 weeks . When ready to bake, pre-heat oven to 400 degrees. Line muffin tins with aluminum liners. Do not stir batter. Fill each cup about 2/3 full. Bake 15 to 20 minutes.

PUMPKIN BREAD
By Susan Stokes

Makes 3 loaves **Serving Size = 1/16 Loaf or 1 Slice** **79 Calories** **2 Fat Grams**

Spicy and moist, just not oily! This recipe makes 3 loaves.

1	egg plus 4 egg whites *	1 tsp.	baking soda
2 1/4 cups	fructose	2 tsp.	baking powder
3 Tbl.	Canola oil (cold pressed)	1/2 tsp.	cloves
2 cups	pumpkin	2 tsp.	cinnamon
2/3 cup	plain non-fat yogurt or applesauce	1/2 tsp.	nutmeg
		1/2 tsp.	ginger
2 tsp.	vanilla	1/2 cup	walnuts or pecans, finely
2 cups	w.w. flour		chopped (measure after
1 1/2 cups	all purpose flour		chopping)
1 tsp.	salt		

  *** or** use 5 egg whites

Preheat oven to 350 degrees. Prepare 3 (8 1/2 x 4 1/2 x 2 1/2) inch loaf pans by greasing and flouring bottoms, or spraying with Bakers Joy. In a large bowl, beat egg and egg whites, beat in fructose. Add oil, pumpkin, yogurt, and vanilla; stir to blend (mixture will look curdled). Stir or sift dry ingredients together, add to pumpkin mixture along with nuts. Stir just until moistened - do not over mix! Divide evenly among the prepared pans. Bake 45 to 60 minutes, or until a toothpick comes out clean. Cool 10 minutes on wire racks, remove from pans and cool completely before wrapping. Freezes well.

Sometimes I add 1 cup of plumped raisins along with the nuts.

NOTES

PUMPKIN CARROT MUFFINS
By Gloria Woodward

BREADS

Serves 24		Serving Size = 1 Muffin		123 Calories		Fat Gram = t

2 cups	carrots - finely grated	1 cup	raisins
2 cups	pumpkin	1 cup	non-fat yogurt
4	egg whites	3 cups	whole grain flour
1 cup	brown sugar	2 tsp.	soda
4 tsp.	baking powder	1 tsp.	salt
2 tsp.	cinnamon		

Spray muffin tins with non-stick cooking spray or use paper muffin cups. Pour batter into the muffin tins and bake at 375 degrees for 13 minutes.

PUMPKIN MUFFINS
By Susan Stokes

Makes 18		Serving Size = 3" muffins		114 Calories		1.5 Fat Grams

Wonderful spicy flavor - these are very nice muffins!

1 cup	w.w. flour	4	egg whites, slightly beaten
1 cups	all purpose flour	1/2 tsp.	vanilla
1 tsp.	baking soda	1/3 cup	plain non-fat yogurt
1/2 tsp.	baking powder	2 Tbl.	margarine
1/2 tsp.	salt	2 Tbl.	honey
1/2 tsp.	cinnamon	2/3 cup	fructose
1/2 tsp.	nutmeg	1 cup	pumpkin
1/4 tsp.	ginger	1/2 cup	raisins

Preheat oven to 400 degrees. Line muffin tins with aluminum liners, or grease bottoms only. Stir dry ingredients together in a large bowl. Stir egg whites, vanilla, yogurt, melted margarine, honey, fructose and pumpkin together, add to dry ingredients; stir just until moistened. Fold in raisins. Fill muffin tins 2/3 full of batter. Bake 17 to 18 minutes, or until a toothpick comes out clean.

NOTES

WHOLE WHEAT BREAD
By EAT & Be Lean ™

Makes 6 Loaves   **Serving Size = 1 slice**   **Calories**   **Fat Grams = 1**
16 slices per loaf

This recipe takes approximately 15 minutes using 2 mixers or 25 minutes by hand. Making bread by hand can be very theroputic.

6 cups	water, warm	2 heaping Tbl.	yeast
1/4 cup	oil	1/3 cup	honey
4 cups	w.w. flour		

Mix the above ingredients together for about 3 minutes. ADD:

2 Tbl.	salt	1/3 cup	w.w. gluten
8 - 10 cups	w.w. flour (approximately)		

Add flour untiol dough pulls away from sides of bowl. Dough should be a little sticky, but workable. Knead for 10 minutes if using a mixer or 15 - 20 minutes by hand. Let dough rest on cupboard for a few minutes. make loaves and place in leaf pans. Put in warm (150 degree) oven and let raise for about 15 minutes. Raise oven temperature to 350 and finish baking for 20 - 30 minutes.

NOTE: You may let the loaves raise on a 150 degree oven with the door propped open with a couple of hot pads. This takes abou5 1/2 hour.

ZUCCHINI BREAD
By Susan Stokes

Makes 2 loaves   **Serving Size = 1 Slice**   **107 Calories**   **2 Fat Grams**
(16 slices per loaf)   **(1 FG with no nuts)**

This bread is so simple to make. When you have lots of zucchini in your garden, be sure to make extra loaves to freeze. Slightly spicy, moist, good bread! This recipe makes 2 loaves.

2 Tbl.	honey		
1 1/3 cups	fructose	2 tsp.	baking powder
3Tbl.	Canola oil (cold pressed)	1 tsp.	baking soda
1	egg plus 2 egg whites	1 tsp.	salt
3 cups	shredded zucchini	1 tsp.	cinnamon
	(I like unpeeled)	1 tsp.	cloves
1/2 cup	plain non-fat yogurt or	1 tsp.	ginger
	applesauce	1/4 cup	finely chopped walnuts or
2 tsp.	vanilla		pecans (measure before
1 1/2 cups	w.w. flour		chopping)
1 1/2 cups	all purpose flour	1 cup	raisins

Preheat oven to 350 degrees. Prepare two 8 1/2 x 4 1/2 x 2 1/2 inch loaf pans by spraying with Bakers Joy, or greasing and flouring the bottoms. In a medium bowl combine the honey, fructose and oil -stir together well, add the egg and egg whites, zucchini, yogurt and vanilla; blend and set aside. In a large bowl, combine all of the dry ingredients, stir well, add nuts and raisins and stir to coat them with flour. Pour in the liquid ingredients, stir until everything is well mixed, but don't over mix. Pour into the prepared pans. Bake for 45 to 60 minutes. Cool on wire rack for 10 minutes, remove from pans, and cool completely before wrapping. Freezes very well.

BREAKFAST

BREAKFAST IDEAS

BEST EVER PANCAKES
By Vicki Robison

Serves 20   **Serving Size = 2 Pancakes**   **114 Calories**   **.5 Fat Grams**

2 cups	mixed whole grain flour (wheat, barley & oat are my favorites)
1 tsp.	baking powder (Rumford brand preferred)
1 tsp.	baking soda
1 Tbl.	honey
3	egg whites
1/2 cup	non-fat plain yogurt *
2 cups	skim milk

Alternative: you can substitute 2 1/2 cups buttermilk in place of yogurt & skim milk.

Mix together and cook on hot griddle. Serve with favorite fruit sauce.

*****Fruit** flavored yogurts can be used as well, but omit honey as fruit yogurts are already sweetened.

BREAKFAST COMPOTE
By Susan Stokes

Serves 6   **Serving Size = 1/3 Cup**   **173 Calories**   **0 Fat Grams**

Put the following into a med. bowl

1 cup	dried, pitted prunes, 6 oz. (cut in 1/2)
1 cup	dried apricots, 6 oz. (cut in 1/2)
1 1/2 cups	Dole Pineapple, Orange, Guava juice
	frozen concentrate (mix as directed on can)

Other juice suggestions:
Pineapple/Orange/Banana
Pineapple/Passion Fruit/Banana
Pineapple/Orange

Stir, cover and refrigerate at least 12 hours. Stir once or twice

CRACKED WHEAT or MULTI-GRAIN CEREAL
By Gloria Woodward

Serves 1   **Serving Size = 1 Cup**   **1 90 Calories**   **1 Fat Gram**

Bring to a boil:

1 cup	water	1/4 tsp.	salt

Stir in: 1/3 cup cracked kernals. Reduce heat to low, stirring a few times. Cover and steam as for rice about 15 - 20 minutes. Serve hot with milk and honey.

FRENCH TOAST
By Susan Stokes

Serves 10   **Serving Size = 1 Slice**   **87 Calories**   **1 Fat Grams**

1/4 cup	skim evaporated milk	1/8 tsp.	salt
1	egg plus 3 egg whites	1/2 tsp.	vanilla
2 tsp.	fructose	10 slices	whole grain bread
1/4 tsp.	cinnamon		
4 tsp.	Butter Buds		

Whisk milk, egg and whites, sugar, cinnamon, Butter Buds, salt and vanilla together. Dip bread into mixture. Fry on a non-stick griddle or fry pan until browned on both sides.

GOOD MORNING WHEAT CEREAL
By Susan Stokes

Serves 6   **Serving Size = 1 1/2 Cups**   **213 Calories**   **.6 Fat Grams**

1 1/2 cup	bulgur wheat
1/3 cup	raisins
1/3 cup	dried apricots cut into small pieces (try other dried fruits also)
1/2 tsp.	salt
3 cups	boiling water

Stir all ingredients together in medium bowl. Cover tightly.   Leave on counter over night. Serve at room temperature or reheat in microwave.

GRANOLA
By Susan Stokes

Serves 12   **Serving Size = 1/2 Cup**   **465 Calories**   **2.8 Fat Grams**

This is a very good recipe for granola. Enjoy!
Preheat oven to 325 degrees.

1 medium	ripe banana - mash and mix with oil, honey, vanilla and cinnamon	3 1/3 cups	old fashioned rolled oats
		3/4 cup	Grapenuts
		1 cup	raisins
1 Tbl.	oil	1/2 cup	dried, diced apricots
1/2 tsp.	vanilla	1/2 cup	dried, diced prunes
1/3 cup	honey	1 tsp.	finely grated orange peel (opt.)
1 tsp.	cinamon		

Add to banana mixture; stuir until thoroughly combine. Spray 15 x 10 x 1 inch jelly roll pan with PAM. Spread oats evenly in pan. Bake 30 - 35 minutes stirring every 10 minutes. Remove, stir in fruits and orange peel - cool - store air tight.

INDIVIDUAL BREAKFAST CUPS

By Susan Stokes

Makes 12	Serving Size = 1 cup	119 Calories	2 Fat Gram

4 cups	cooked* brown rice, 4 grain mix, or bulgur	1/3 cup	skim milk
2 oz.	Kraft Light Naturals sharp cheddar cheese, shreded (1/2 cup lightly packed)	2 large 2 large 1/4 tsp. 1/4 - 1/2 tsp.	egg egg whites salt pepper
2 oz.	Frigo Truly Lite mozzarella cheese, shredded (1/2 cup lightly packed)		or 4 Egg Beaters

Preheat oven to 400 degrees. Spray a 12 cup muffin tin with cooking spray. Whisk egg, egg whites, salt, pepper and milk together in a large bowl. Combine cheeses and cooked grain. Stir to combine. Divide mixture evenly into the prepared muffin cups. Sprinkle with paprika if desired. Bake for 15 to 18 minutes or until set.

Variation: Spray a small non-stick fry pan with cooking spray. Saute until barely tender, 3 tablespoons each, finely chopped red bell pepper and sliced green onion. Add along with 1 can (4 oz.) drained diced green chiles, and 1/4 to 1/2 teaspoon ground cumin. Serve with Salsa.

Individual Breakfast Cups can be frozen. To reheat, microwave each cup for 1 minute on full power.

* I like to cook extra rice at dinner time, then I can put this together quickly in the morning.

MENU SUGGESTION

W	12 oz.	
V	V-8 juice	
F	Fresh Fruit	
G	Whole Grain Toast	
P	INDIVIDUAL BREAKFAST CUP	

MUESLI

By Susan Stokes

Serves 4	Serving Size = 1 cup	254 Calories	2 Fat Grams

8 oz.	Non-fat flavored yogurt or 1 cup plain - sweetened to taste with honey	1/2 tsp. 1/3 cup 1/3 cup 1 medium	grated lemon peel raisins diced dried apricots apple, unpeeled and diced
1 cup	dry rolled oats		
1/4 cup	Grapenuts		
4 tsp.	almond slice		

OPTIONAL:

1 cup	pineapple tidbits
1	banana, sliced
1 cup	orange sections

Mix yogurt, oats, lemon peel, dried fruit, and apple together. Let stand for 10 minutes. Divide into 4 bowls, sprinkle each with 1 tablespoon grapenuts and 1 teaspoon sliced almonds.

NO FAT BLENDER PANCAKES
By Gloria Woodward

Serves 8   **Serving Size = 4, 3" Pancakes**   **103 Calories**   **.5 Fat Gram**

In the blender add:

1 cup	whole wheat kernals (or any combination of grains totaling 1 cup)
1 cup	skim milk

Blend on number 2 or 3 speed for 2 minutes. Add:

1/2 cup	skim milk

Blend an additional 2 min.

During this second 2 minutes add through the funnel:

1/2 tsp.	salt
1 or 2 Tbl.	honey or molasses

After turning off the blender remove the lid and add:

1 Tbl.	Baking Powder
1/2 cup	non-fat plain yogurt

Bake on a hot griddle, 350- 375, sprayed lightly with cooking spray.

Note: The non-fat yogurt replaces the eggs and oil from the original recipe. This same idea can be used in many recipes. Substiture 1/2 to 3/4 cup non-fat yogurt for 1/2 cup oil and 2 eggs. Play with it and find the amount you like best for your favorite recipes!

TIPS: This recipe can be made with buttermilk instead of milk, in which case you would also add 1/4 teaspoon soda OR use 1 1/4 cups water and 1/4 cup dry milk. Another fun variation is to use 2 or three grains whose total equals 1 cup. Two heaping Tablespoons cornmeal added to this recipe is delicious.

OVEN STEAMED WHEAT
By Susan Stokes

Serving Size = 1 Cup   **190 Calories**   **1 Fat Gram**

Preheat oven to 350 degrees. In heavy saucepan or small roaster, combine 2 cups water with each cup whole wheat berries. Add 1/2 teaspoon salt per cup of wheat. Bring to a boil and cook for 5 minutes. Remove from heat, cover tightly. Place in oven. After 10 minutes turn off oven. Leave undisturbed for 10 to 12 hours (good to do over night). Left overs refrigerate or freeze well.

Serve warmed or cold with honey and milk. Add dried fruit bits if desired.

1 cup of dry makes 3 cups of cooked.

Note: Use cooked wheat in casseroles and salads - not just for breakfast.

STRAWBERRY BANANA BLENDER BREAKFAST DRINK
By Susan Stokes

Serves 2   **Serving Size = 1 1/2 Cup**   **238 Calories**   **Fat Grams = t**

Put into blender container:

2 cups	cold skim milk
1 1/2 cups	individually frozen strawberries
1 large	**ripe** banana
2 Tbl.	orange or pineapple juice concentrate
1 Tbl.	fructose

Blend on high speed until smooth and creamy.

WHOLE WHEAT PANCAKES
By Susan Stokes

Serves 10   **Serving Size = 2**   **110 Calories**   **1 Fat Gram**

2 cups	whole wheat flour		
4 tsp.	fructose	3	egg whites
1/2 tsp.	salt	1 cup	non-fat yogurt
1/2 tsp.	baking soda	1 1/2 cups	club soda or skim milk
1/2 tsp.	baking powder	2 tsp.	vegetable oil

In a large bowl, stir dry ingredients together. Whisk egg whites, yogurt and club soda together. Add liquids to dry ingredients and blend with a wire whisk just enough to moisten. Dip out batter with a 1/4 cup measuring cup. Bake on a non-stick griddle. Turn only once.

Note: Krusteaz Whole Wheat & Honey Pancake Mix is better to use than bleached, enriched white pancake mix when in a hurry. You just add water. There is 1 gram of fat in three, 4 inch pancakes.

  * I add 1/3 cup dry oatmeal to each cup of dry mix and use Club Soda to replace water.

WHOLE WHEAT WAFFLES
By EAT & Be Lean

Makes 4   **Serving Size = 1 Large Waffle**   **174 Calories**   **4 Fat Grams**

4	egg whites (beaten)	1 cup	w.w. flour
1 1/4 cup	skim milk	3 tsp.	baking powder
1 Tbl.	oil	1/2 tsp.	salt

Sift dry ingredients. Mix water and milk together. Add oil and dry ingredients and beat until smooth. Beat egg whites until stiff. Fold in beaten egg whites. Bake in a preheated waffle iron. As an option, add 1 tablespoon honey (16 FG per waffle) before blending in the eggs. **Serve** with fresh, frozen or pureed fruit.

DESSERTS

DESSERTS

The Dessert recipes have been rated to help you determine the type of treat you want.

A = No fat - low sugar   **C** = Low fat - high sugar
B = Low fat - low sugar   **D** = High fat - high sugar

APPLESAUCE CAKE
By Susan Stokes

Serves 18   **Serving Size = 2"x3" piece**   **165 Calories**   **2 Fat Grams**

Easy to make. Moist and spiced just right.

Preheat oven to 375 degrees. Spray a 9" x 13" pan with non-stick cooking spray, or grease and flour. Stir the following ingredients together in a large bowl:

2 cups	w.w. flour		
2/3 cups	all purpose flour	1 tsp.	baking powder
2/3 cup	fructose	1 tsp.	cinnamon
1 tsp.	baking soda	1/2 tsp.	cloves
1 tsp.	salt	1/2 tsp.	allspice

Whisk the following ingredients together; add to the dry ingredients. Mix until well blended.

1/3 cup	brown sugar	1 3/4 cups	applesauce (16 oz. can)
1/2 cup	apple juice concentrate	2 Tbl.	Canola oil (cold pressed)
1	egg plus 2 whites	1 cup	raisins

Stir in raisins. Pour into prepared pan. Bake 55 to 60 minutes. Serve plain, dusted with powdered sugar, or glazed with the CREAM CHEESE GLAZE^ .

NOTE: If walnuts are added be sure to add 9 grams of fat for every 2 tablespoons of nuts.

BANANA "POUND" CAKE
By Susan Stokes

Serves 24   **Serving Size = 1 1/4" Slice**   **132 Calories**   **1 Fat Grams**

This cake is moist but not oily like the pound cakes I used to make. Wonderful delicate flavor and texture.

1 pkg.	Pillsbury Lovin Lites yellow cake mix
3 1/2 oz. pkg.	banana cream instant pudding mix
1/4 cup	flour
3/4 cup	mashed banana
6	egg whites
2/3 cup	plain nonfat yogurt or applesauce
2/3 cup	water

Glaze

1 cup	powdered sugar	1/4 tsp.	banana extract
2 Tbl.	hot water	1/2 tsp.	vanilla extract

Preheat oven to 375 degrees. Spray 10 inch Bundt or tube pan with Bakers Joy or grease and flour. Combine all ingredients in large mixer bowl. Blend; then beat at medium speed for 2 minutes. Pour into prepared pan; cut through batter with a butter knife to remove air pockets. Bake 50 to 55 minutes, until pick comes out clean. Cool in pan on a rack for 15 minutes. Remove from pan and finish cooling on a rack. Stir glaze ingredients together until smooth. Drizzle with glaze.

DESSERTS

BANANA SPLIT
By Susan Stokes

Bananas
Vanilla Frozen Yogurt - Non-fat is preferable. Read the label on store brands, or purchase at your local Yogurt Shop, or make your own.

ASSORTED TOPPINGS
Dream Whip or Marshmallow Creme
Read labels to find the best topping:

	AMOUNT	FAT GRAMS	CALORIES
Pineapple topping	2 Tbl.	0.2	100
Strawberry topping	2 Tbl.	0.1	100
Caramel or Butterscotch	2 Tbl.	0.1	120
Marshmallow Creme	1 Tbl.	0.0	60
Dream Whip	1 Tbl.	1.0	10
Sliced Almonds	1 Tbl.	3.0	50
Hershey Chocolate Syrup (dark brown label)	2 Tbl.	0.4	80

Smuckers and Mrs. Richardsen both make light fat hot fudge toppings.

REMEMBER: All of the toppings are still high in sugar.

BREAD-CRUMB COOKIES
By Gloria Woodward

With Nuts **Makes 5 Dozen**	**Serving Size = 1 Cookie**	**60 Calories**	**2 Fat Gram**
Without Nuts **Makes 5 Dozen**	**Serving Size = 1 Cookie**	**54 Calories**	**1 Fat Gram**

Place broken pieces of stale bread in blender, jog a few times, then blend on speed 1 until fine crumbs.

Place the following ingredients in your large bowl with the kneading arm in place.

3 cups	whole wheat bread crumbs	4	egg whites
3/4 cup	applesauce	2 cups	whole wheat flour
2 cups	raisins or other dried fruit	2 tsp.	baking soda
1/4 cup	cooking oil	2 tsp.	cinnamon
1/2 cup	honey	1 tsp.	allspice
1/2 cup	non-fat yogurt	1/2 cup	nuts

Mix well. Drop by spoonful onto greased baking sheet. Bake in oven at 350 degrees for 10 minutes. Whole wheat cookies should appear under-done. Makes 5 dozen.

With the nutes included each cookie has 1 1/2 fat grams. Without nuts only one fat gram each.

DESSERTS

BROILED PINEAPPLE ROUNDS
By Susan Stokes

Serves 1 **Serving Size = 1 Slice** **51 Calories** **0 Fat Grams**

3/4 inch   thick fresh pineapple slices or canned in juice slices
1 Tbl.   brown sugar per pineapple slice

Spray a broiler-proof with cooking spray. Arrange pineapple slices in the broiler-proof dish. Sprinkle 1 tablespoon brown sugar over each slice of pineapple. Broil 5 inches from heat until hot nd bubbly.

VARIATIONS:

Try a combination of canned or fesh pear chunks, pineapple chunks, orange sections, or drained mandarin arange sections, and banana chunks. Spray a broiler-proof dish with cooking spray. Toss fruit together and arrange in broiler dish. Sprinkle with brown sugar and dust with cinnamon. Broil until the sugar bubbles. Serve hot over nonfat vanilla frozen yogurt or vanilla fat free frozen dessert.

CARROT CAKE
By Susan Stokes

Serves 18 **Serving Size = 2"x 3" piece** **168 Calories** **3 Fat Grams**

This was a challenge, but I am glad I made the effort! The cake is moist but not oily, with all the flavor of the original recipe. Each serving of cake with frosting used to have 25 grams of fat. I give three different ideas for topping the cake - all very different, but delicious. See the next page.

1 cup	w.w. flour	3/4 cup	fructose
1 cup	all purpose flour	2 tsp.	vanilla
2 tsp.	baking powder	3 Tbl.	vegetable oil
1 tsp.	baking soda	2	eggs plus 2 egg whites
2 tsp.	cinnamon	3 cups	grated carrot
1/2 tsp.	allspice	1 cup	applesauce or plain nonfat
1/2 tsp.	salt		yogurt
1 cup	raisins	1 cup	drained crushed pineapple
1/3 cup	firmly packed brown sugar		

Nuts are optional, see Note

Preheat oven to 350 degrees. Spray a 9 x 13 inch pan with Bakers Joy, or grease and flour. Combine all of the dry ingredients in a large bowl, stir well; stir in raisins and set aside. Combine brown sugar, fructose, vanilla, and oil, stir well, add egg and egg whites; beat mixture with an electric mixer or a wire whisk. Stir in carrots, applesauce, and drained pineapple. Add liquid mixture to dry ingredients. Mix well. Pour into prepared pan. Bake for 50 to 55 minutes, or until toothpick comes out clean. Cool completely on a wire rack.

Note: If you decide to add walnuts or pecans add 9 grams of fat for every 2 Tablespoons of nuts you add.

CARROT CAKE TOPPINGS

CREAM CHEESE GLAZE

Makes 1 Cup		953 Calories	12 Fat Grams
4 oz.	fat free cream cheese	2 cups	sifted powdered sugar
1 Tbl.	butter	1 tsp.	vanilla
		1/4 tsp.	finely grated orange peel

Beat cream cheese, margarine, and vanilla until smooth. Add powdered sugar, beat until smooth; stir in orange peel. Chill while cake is baking and cooling. (This has a more runny consistency than standard cream cheese frostings - additional powdered sugar does not make it more solid.)

Carrot cake with cream cheese glaze - 18 servings and 4 grams fat each.

VANILLA TOPPING
Entire recipe = 601 calories and 17 Fat Grams

1/2 cup	skim evaporated milk or	1 1/2 Tbl.	butter
	buttermilk	1 Tbl.	honey
4 tsp.	Butter Buds	1/2 tsp.	baking soda
1/2 cup	fructose	1 tsp.	vanilla

Put all ingredients except vanilla into a 2 or 3 quart saucepan (mixture foams up during cooking). Bring to a boil, for 5 minutes. Remove from heat, add vanilla. Pour evenly over cake 10 minutes after it comes from the oven.

Carrot cake with topping - 18 servings - 4 grams fat per serving.

ORANGE GLAZE
Entire Recipe = 542 Calories and 4 Fat Grams

2/3 cup	fructose	pinch of	salt
1/4 cup	cornstarch	1 tsp.	finely grated orange peel
1 cup	orange juice	1 tsp.	salt
1 tsp.	lemon juice	1 tsp.	butter

Stir fructose and cornstarch together in a small saucepan. Add orange and lemon juice, orange peel and butter. Cook over medium heat until thick and glossy. Cool and spread on cake.

Carrot cake with Orange glaze - 18 servings - 3 grams of fat per serving.

NOTES

DESSERTS

"CHEESECAKE" PIE
By Susan Stokes

Serves 8	Serving Size = 1/8 th of a pie	232 Calories	2 Fat Grams

9"	graham cracker crust	1/4 cup	lemon juice
8 oz.	fat free cream cheese	1 tsp.	vanilla
1 cup	homemade SWEETENED	canned	lite cherry pie filling
	CONDENSED MILK^	1/2 tsp.	Almond extract
		1/2 tsp.	finely grated lemon peel

Put sweetened condensed milk, cream cheese, lemon juice, and vanilla in blender container, blend until smooth. Pour into pie shell. Chill 2 or 3 hours until set. Stir almond extract into cherry filling, spoon on top of pie. This tastes great topped with fresh fruit or berries.

GRAHAM CRACKER CRUST

Serving Size = 1 crust	586 Calories	16 Fat Grams

1 1/4 cup	graham cracker crumbs (8 full crackers)
1 Tbl.	fructose
2 Tbl.	Promise Ultra (light tube margarine - 4 FG per Tbl.)
2 tsp.	water

Melt margarine, stir into crumbs and sugar. Sprinkle water over mixture and stir together until evenly moistened, Press onto bottom and side of a 9" pie plate sprayed with cooking spray. Bake at 350 degrees for 8 to 10 minutes, until just starting to lightly brown. Cool before filling.

SWEETENED CONDENSED MILK

Makes 3 Cups	Serving Size = 1 Cup	621 Calories	2 Fat Grams

1 cup	very hot tap water
4 cups	instant non-fat powdered milk
1 1/2 cups	fructose
1 Tbl.	Promise Ultra tub margarine
4 tsp.	Butter Buds

Put hot water and powdered milk into blender container, process briefly, turn off and scrape down sides of container. Process again, turn off and scrape sides again to make sure all of the powdered milk is dissolved. Turn the blender back on, and add the fructose through the opening in the lid while it is running. Turn off, scrape sides, blend again. Pour into a quart jar, or other container. Cover and refrigerate over night before using.

CHERRY BERRY TRIFLE
By Susan Stokes

Serves 18 **Serving Size = 2/3 Cup** **187 Calories** **1 Fat Gram**

A very easy variation of an old classic dessert. Vary it by using other kinds of fruit.

1 envelope	Dream Whip	16 oz. can	cherry pie filling
3.4 oz. pkg.	instant vanilla pudding mix (use skim milk with mix)	2 cups	whole berry cranberry sauce
1 tsp.	almond extract	2 Tbl.	sliced almonds
9"	ANGEL FOOD CAKE^ or 10 oz. loaf of cake torn into 1" pieces		

Prepare Dream Whip as directed on package. Prepare vanilla pudding mix as directed on package. Fold Dream Whip and almond extract into pudding. Stir pie filling and cranberry sauce together. In a 3 quart serving bowl (clear gloss is very pretty) alternate three layers each of cake pieces, fruit filling and pudding. Sprinkle toasted almonds in a circle about 1 1/2 inches in from edge of the bowl. Cover with plastic wrap and refrigerate at least 5 hours before serving. This is a great dessert to make the day before you want to serve it.

Vary flavor by using blueberry pie filling or fold 2 cups fresh or frozen raspberries (drained) into 3/4 cup all fruit raspberry jam.

CHERRY CHOCOLATE BARS
By Susan Stokes

Serves 15 **Serving Size = 2 1/2" x 3"** **169 Calories** **2 Fat Grams**
(Not including yogurt)

Quick and easy!

1 pkg.	Pillsbury Lovin Lites Devils Food cake mix	3	egg whites
21 oz. can	cherry pie filling	1 tsp.	almond extract

Preheat oven to 350 degrees. Spray a 9 x 13 inch pan with Bakers Joy, or lightly grease and flour. Put all ingredients into a large bowl, stir until well mixed. Spread in prepared pan. Bake 30 to 35 minutes. Cool before cutting. Serve with a small scoop of non-fat vanilla yogurt drizzled with Smuckers Light Hot Fudge Topping.

NOTES

DESSERTS

CHEWY DATE MACAROONS
By Susan Stokes

Makes 3 dozen **Serving Size = 1 cookie** **20 Calories** **Fat Grams = t**

2	egg whites (from large eggs)	1 cup	crushed cornflake crumbs
1/4 tsp.	salt	3/4 cup	oat bran
1 tsp.	vanilla	1/2 cup	chopped dates
2/3 cup	packed brown sugar	1/4 cup	finely chopped, drained well, maraschino cherries

Preheat oven to 350 degrees. Line baking sheets with foil; lightly spray with cooking spray. Beat egg whites and salt until foamy. Gradually add brown sugar; beat until stiff. Fold in cornflake crumbs, oat bran, dates and cherries. Drop by rounded teaspoonfuls two inches apart onto prepared baking sheets. Bake 9 to 12 minutes or until lightly browned. Immediately remove from baking sheets.

CHOCOLATE CHEWS
By Susan Stokes

Makes 6 dozen **Serving Size = 2" cookie** **45 Calories** **1 Fat Gram**

Chewy chocolate crackle top cookies, especially for chocoholics who want to eat low-fat and still have an occasional chocolate treat. Hershey's European style cocoa is very nice in these!

6 Tbl.	butter or margarine	2 1/3 cups	flour
1 3/4 cups	sugar	6 Tbl.	cocoa
2 tsp.	vanilla	2 tsp.	baking powder
3	large egg whites	1/2 tsp.	salt
as desired	powdered sugar for coating cookie dough		

Cream the butter, sugar and vanilla. Beat in egg whites one at a time, beating between each addition. Stir or sift all of the dry ingredients together; add to creamed mixture. Beat until all ingredients are well blended. Cover and chill at least 3 hours (This is a soft dough, so I usually make it the day before I want to bake it). Form into small balls (I used a #100 ice cream dipper, which holds 1 1/2 teaspoons). Roll in powdered sugar, place on lightly greased baking sheet. Bake at 350 degrees 10 to 12 minutes - I like these chewy, so I bake them 10 minutes.

NOTES

CHOCOLATE CHIP COOKIES
By Susan Stokes

Makes 2 1/2 Dozen   **Serving Size = 1 Cookie**   **52 Calories**   **1.3 Fat Grams**

Lower Fat Version

1/3 cup	packed brown sugar	1/2 cup	w.w. flour
3 Tbl.	granulated sugar	1/2 cup	all purpose flour
1 Tbl.	light corn syrup	1/2 tsp.	baking soda
2 Tbl.	butter or margarine	1/4 tsp.	salt
4 tsp.	Butter Buds	1/3 cup	miniature semisweet
1 tsp.	vanilla		chocolate chips (2 oz.)
2	egg whites	1 cup	crispy rice cereal

Preheat oven to 375 degrees.

Cream sugars, corn syrup, butter or margarine, Butter Buds, and vanilla in a medium size mixing bowl. Add egg white and combine thoroughly.
Sift or stir flour, soda, and salt together. Add to creamed mixture; stir to combine. Stir in miniature chocolate chips and cereal. Drop by rounded teaspoonfuls onto ungreased baking sheets. Bake 7 to 9 minutes. Cool slightly; remove to a wire rack to finish cooling. Store in an airtight container.

CHOCOLATE FIX
By Susan Stokes

Serves 12   **Serving Size = 2" x 2 1/2"**   **88 Calories**   **2 Fat Grams**

Fudge like brownies with a very intense chocolate taste!

2 Tbl.	butter or margarine	4 large	egg whites
1/4 cup	plain non-fat yogurt	1/2 cup	flour
1 cup	sugar	1/4 tsp.	Salt
1/3 cup	Hershey's European style cocoa	1 1/2 tsp.	Vanilla

Preheat oven to 350 degrees. Line an eight inch square baking pan with tin foil; spray with Bakers Joy or grease and flour. Put all ingredients into a medium size mixing bowl; beat with an electric beater until batter is smooth. Pour into prepared pan. Bake 30 minutes (top should look set - do not over bake). Cool completely on a wire rack. Lift foil out of pan, dust top of brownies with powdered sugar, and cut into 12 pieces. (Use a long sharp knife, and wipe the blade clean after each cut.)

NOTES

DESSERTS

CHOCOLATE-MINT SENSATION
By Susan Stokes

Serves 12   **Serving Size = 2" square**   **360 Calories**   **3 Fat Grams**

1 pkg.	BETTY CROCKER Light Fudge Brownie Mix
1 quart	Fat Free Frozen Yogurt (vanilla flavor)
2 oz.	crushed peppermint candy cane
	(red, white & green is prettiest)
	Low Fat Hot Fudge Topping
	Dream Whip Topping (prepared with skim milk)

Make brownies according to package directions. Cool completely. Soften frozen yogurt slightly; stir in 1/4 cup crushed candy and re-freeze.

TO SERVE: Cut brownies into 24 two inch squares - wipe knife blade between each cut. Layer in small dessert dishes: brownie, 1/3 cup size scoop of frozen yogurt, another brownie, 1 tablespoon warmed topping, 1 tablespoon Dream Whip, sprinkle of additional crushed candy.

VARIATIONS: Brownie with Vanilla Frozen Yogurt and Cherry Pie Filling or brownie with Fudge Ripple Frozen Yogurt and Kraft Caramel Topping (12.5 oz. squeeze bottle)

CHOCO-MINT MALT
By Susan Stokes

Serves 3   **Serving Size = 1 Cup**   **364 Calories**   **0 Fat Grams**

1 cup	vanilla nonfat frozen yogurt	1 1/ cup	skim milk
1 Tbl.	malted milk powder	1 Tbl.	choco flavored syrup
4	starlight mint candies	5	ice cubes

Combine all ingredients in blender container. Cover and process until smooth. Serve immediately.

Variation: Leave out mint candies and add 1/2 teaspoon vanilla extract.

CHOCO-MINT PUDDING
By Susan Stokes

Serves 4   **Serving Size = 1/2 Cup**   **165 Calories**   **1.5 Fat Grams**

When you are craving chocolate, have this instead of a bar or handful of chocolate chips - chocolate flavor and mouth feel - much less fat!

1 pkg.	chocolate instant pudding	4 Tbl.	Dream Whip topping
2 cups	skim milk	2 tsp.	grated chocolate (milk
2	drops peppermint extract		chocolate or semi sweet)

Prepare pudding with milk and peppermint extract. Spoon into 4 dessert dishes; top each with 1 tablespoon Dream Whip and 1/2 teaspoon grated chocolate.

Black Forest Variation: Layer the chocolate pudding and cherry pie filling with a little almond extract stirred in, top with Dream Whip.

COCOA KISSES
By Susan Stokes

Makes 5 dozen   **Serving Size = 2 Cookies**   **32 Calories**   **.5 Fat Grams**

This cookie recipe is meringue based. They are crisp on the outside, and chewy in the middle. These cookies are best if eaten within 2 or 3 days of being baked. They freeze well if longer storage is desired.

2 egg	whites (from large eggs)	2/3 cup	granulated sugar
1/8 tsp.	salt	1/2 cup	saltine cracker crumbs
1/2 tsp.	vanilla	2 Tbl.	cocoa
1/4 tsp.	cream of tartar	3 Tbl.	mini chocolate chips

Preheat oven to 300 degrees. Line baking sheets with tin foil and spray lightly with cooking spray.

Beat egg whites until frothy. Add salt, vanilla, and cream of tartar; continue beating while adding sugar. When the mixture is quite stiff, fold cracker crumbs, cocoa, and mini chips in gently.

Drop by teaspoonfuls onto prepared baking sheets. Bake about 20 minutes. Let cool on the pans for 1 or 2 minutes. Carefully remove to finish cooling on a wire rack. When cool, store in a tightly closed container.

Cocoa-Mint Kisses - add 2 tablespoons finely crushed candy cane or starlight mint candy.

COOL PERFECTION CAKE
By Susan Stokes

Serves 18   **Serving Size = 2"x3" Piece**   **180 Calories**   **2 Fat Grams**

Yummy! Sometimes I spread 1/3 of the frosting on the cake and put a layer of well drained fruit on top; (such as sliced strawberries) swirl on remaining frosting.

3 oz. pkg.	flavored gelatin (strawberry, lemon, orange pineapple black cherry etc.)
1 cup	Shasta soda pop in matching flavor (strawberry, lemon-lime, orange, black cherry etc.)
1	Pillsbury Loven Lites White Cake mix

Frosting

1 envelope	Dream Whip	1 1/2 cups	cold skim milk
3.4 oz. pkg.	instant vanilla pudding mix	1 tsp.	vanilla

Fruit for garnish if desired

Bring Shasta to a boil, stir into gelatin; stir until gelatin is dissolved. Set aside at room temperature.

Prepare cake mix according to the recipe on the back of the box. Bake in a 9 x 13 x 2 inch pan. Cool cake in the pan for 25 minutes. Poke deep holes in the cake about 1/2 inch apart, slowly pour the gelatin/soda mixture over the cake. Refrigerate.

Combine Dream Whip, instant pudding mix, cold skim milk, and vanilla in a deep bowl. Beat with an electric mixer until stiff. (about 8 minutes) Frost cake immediately. Cake must be refrigerated; it can be frozen. Garnish with fresh fruit if desired.

DESSERTS

CRANBERRY AND PEAR COBBLER
By Susan Stokes

Serves 8   **Serving Size = 2/3 Cup Fruit**   **217 Calories**   **3 Fat Grams**
1 Biscuit

FRUIT

2 cans	lite pears, sliced, drained (16 oz.)	
12-oz. bag	cranberries (3 cups)	
2 Tbl.	quick-cooking tapioca	
1-1/2 tsp.	grated orange peel	
1 cup	fructose	
3/4 cup	orange juice	

BISCUIT TOPPING

3/4 cup	whole wheat flour
1/4 cup	all-purpose flour
1 tsp.	baking powder
1/2 tsp.	salt
1/4 tsp.	cream of tarter
1/4 tsp.	baking soda
2 Tbl.	fructose
2 Tbl.	margarine
2/3 cup	plain non-fat yogurt

Preheat oven to 425 degrees. In deep 2 1/2 quart baking dish, mix pears, cranberries, tapioca, orange peel, fructose, and orange juice. Cover and bake 20 minutes, stirring occasionally. After cranberry mixture has baked 15 minutes, prepare cobbler topping: In medium bowl, with fork, mix flours, baking powder, salt, cream of tarter, baking soda, and 2 tablespoons fructose. Cut in margarine until mixture resembles coarse crumbs. Stir yogurt into flour mixture until just moistened. Remove cranberry mixture from oven and uncover. Spoon cobbler topping onto cranberry mixture into 8 mounds. Bake 15 minutes or until topping is golden brown and cranberry mixture is bubbly and slightly thickened. Serve warm or cold, topped with nonfat frozen vanilla yogurt.

CRANBERRY ORANGE UPSIDE-DOWN CAKE
By Susan Stokes

Serves 8   **Serving Size = 1/8th Slice**   **270 Calories**   **2 Fat Grams**

Pretty and so tasty! Bake the other half of the batter and freeze to use later with FRUIT COCKTAIL SAUCE^ or for Strawberry Shortcake.

Preheat oven to 350 degrees. Grease bottom and 1/2 inch up sides of a 9-inch round cake pan with 1 tablespoon butter. Lightly grease and flour another 9-inch pan for the other half of the batter.

1 cup	whole berry cranberry sauce	1/4 cup	flour
1/4 cup	honey	1 1/3 cups	orange juice
1 - 2 tsp.	grated orange rind	3	egg whites
1	Pillsbury Lovin Lites white cake mix		

Mix cranberry sauce, honey, and orange rind; spread in prepared pan. Put cake mix, flour, juice, and egg whites into large mixer bowl. Beat on low speed until moistened, then on high for 2 minutes. Pour half of the batter over the cranberries; pour the rest into the other pan. Bake both cakes 35 to 40 minutes. Cool 5 minutes; turn up side down cake out onto serving plate - if any cranberries stick, spoon them out and onto cake. Serve warm with 1 tablespoon prepared Dream Whip per serving.

CRISPY DESSERT SHELLS
By Susan Stokes

Serve 1	Serving Size = 1 dessert shell	95 Calories	1 Fat Gram

1   Villa Victoria Premium flour tortilla
1 tsp.   Cinnamon/sugar mixture

Spray a plain white paper towel with cooking spray. Lay 1 tortilla on the paper towel; lightly spray tortilla with cooking spray and sprinkle with cinnamon/sugar mixture. Put into microwave for 30 seconds on full power. Remove from microwave and fit into a cereal bowl (paper towel included). Microwave for 45 seconds on full power; rotate and microwave another 30 seconds. Remove from bowl, pull off paper towel, and let dessert shell cool on a rack. (If tortilla puffs up in the middle, stop microwave and poke tortilla with a sharp knife; push down to deflate.)

Note: Make these shells without cinnamon/sugar. Line with a lettuce leaf; try filling with the CALIFORNIA TACO^ recipe in this book to make very low fat Taco Salad.

FILLINGS

Here are just a few ideas - use your imagination and you will come up with many other possibilities!

Serves 1	Serving Size = 1	195 Calories	0 Fat Grams

#1.   1/2 peach (fresh or canned, well drained)
1/3 cup Vanilla Nonfat Frozen Yogurt or Nonfat Frozen Dessert
1 Tbl. Kraft Caramel Topping (look for the 12.5 oz. squeeze bottle)
Wonderful served for dessert after Mexican Food!

Serves 1	Serving Size = 1	190 Calories	0 Fat Grams

#2.   1/3 cup Vanilla Nonfat Frozen Yogurt or Nonfat Frozen Dessert
1/4 cup Warm Apple Pie Filling (cherry or berry pie fillings taste wonderful)

Serves 8	Serving Size = 2" x 4" rectangle	204 Calories	Fat Grams = t

#3.   **Make** low-fat pumpkin pie filling by substituting skim evaporated milk for regular evaporated milk, and 2 egg whites for each egg.

Spray an 8x8 inch square cake pan with cooking spray, pour in pumpkin filling, bake at 350 degrees until set. Cool, cut into squares. Serve in dessert shell with nonfat frozen yogurt, nonfat frozen dessert, or Dream Whip.

#4.   **Use** filling recipe for MATT'S FROZEN PUMPKIN PIE^

NOTES

CRISPY TREATS
By Susan Stokes

Makes 24 bars	Serving Size = 2 1/4" x 2" piece	66 Calories	.5 Fat Grams

Same great taste you remember - less fat!

1 Tbl.	butter
10 oz.	regular size marshmallows (40) OR 4 cups miniature marshmallows
1 tsp.	vanilla
5 cups	crispy rice cereal - OR combination of crispy rice and Total, Corn Flakes, or Rice Bran Flakes.

Line a 9 x 13 inch pan with foil; spray with vegetable cooking spray. Melt butter and marshmallows over low heat, stirring until completely melted (or, to make it easier to handle, melt in Microwave for 2 minutes). Remove from heat; stir in vanilla, then stir in cereal. Press into prepared pan. (I just gave my hand a quick spray with Pam - it worked great!) Cool in pan. Lift foil out, turn crispy treats onto a cutting board; cut into 24 bars. Keep in an air tight container with wax paper between layers.

EASY BAKED APPLES
By Susan Stokes

Serves 4	Serving Size = 1 Apple	117 Calories	.7 Fat Grams

4 medium	baking apples	1/4 cup	apple cider
4 Tbl.	honey or maple syrup	to taste	ground cinnamon

Core apples. With a paring knife or potato peeler, remove a small spiral of peel on the top quarter of each apple. Place apples around the edges of a casserole dish and pour in apple cider. Drizzle each apple with 1 tablespoon honey; dust lightly with cinnamon. Cover with lid; micro on full power for 6 to 7-1/2 minutes, turning dish once. Serve with a dollop of vanilla nonfat yogurt.

VARIATION: Combine 1/4 cup brown sugar, 1/4 teaspoon cinnamon, and 2 tablespoons raisins. Put equal amount of this mixture into each cored apple. Pour cider around apples and proceed as in above recipe for Easy Baked Apples. Serve with custard sauce, if desired.

NOTES

EASY LAYERED DESSERT
By Susan Stokes

Serves 15   **Serving Size = 3" x 2" Piece**   **145 Calories**   **1 Fat Grams**

Be sure to read the labels on the graham cracker boxes - some have more fat in them than others.

15 whole	graham crackers (30 squares)	21 oz. can	lite cherry pie filling
1 cup	plain non-fat yogurt	1/2 tsp.	almond extract
2 cups	skim milk	1/4 tsp.	cinnamon
1 large pkg.	instant vanilla pudding mix (6 oz.)		

Line a 9 x 13 inch pan with 1/2 of the crackers, breaking if necessary. Stir yogurt, milk, pudding mix, and almond extract together, then beat on low speed for 2 minutes. Spread 1/2 of the pudding over the crackers; top with the rest of the crackers, then the rest of the pudding. Stir almond extract and cinnamon into cherry pie filling; spoon evenly over top of the pudding. Chill 3 hours. Cut into squares.

Variation: Blueberry pie filling with 1 teaspoon lemon juice added.

DESSERTS

FILLO TART SHELLS
By Susan Stokes

Serves 1   **Serving Size = 1 Shell**   **32 Calories**   **Fat Grams = t**

Thaw Fillo according to package directions.
Spray a muffin tin with Butter Flavored Pam.
Preheat the oven to 350 degrees.

For each 4 tart shells, use 2 sheets Fillo, stacked. Keep the rest of the Fillo leaves under a damp (not wet) towel. Lightly spray the top sheet of Fillo with Pam. Cut the double sheet into quarters. Fit each double quarter into a muffin cup; turn and fold and crumple excess until tart shell looks attractive. Continue until muffin tin is filled. (If shells are to be used for dessert, you can sprinkle them with sugar, or a combination of cinnamon and sugar.) Bake about 8 minutes, or until a pale golden brown. Fill just before serving.

Note: Fillings for these tart shells are limited only by your imagination. Try Creamed Chicken, Salmon, or Crab (low-fat of course!) For dessert, try fruit fillings such as PINEAPPLE PIE FILLING^, puddings fruit filling etc.

The PINEAPPLE PIE FILLING^ on the next page is excellent.

FILLO TART FILLING

PINEAPPLE PIE FILLING

Serves 10   **Serving Size = 1/3 Cup**   **55 Calories**   **0 Fat Grams**

Stir together in a saucepan:

20 oz. can	crushed pineapple in juice	4 Tbl.	flour
1/3 cup	fresh lemon juice	4 Tbl.	cornstarch
1 cup	fructose	1/2 pkt.	Butter Buds (4 teaspoons)
1/2 tsp.	salt		

Pour crushed pineapple into a 4 cup measuring cup, add lemon juice, then fill to the 4 cup level with water. Stir dry ingredients together in a medium sauce pan. Stir pineapple mixture into the dry ingredients in the saucepan. Cook until thick and bubbly. Lay a piece of plastic wrap or wax paper directly on the surface of the pie filling. Cool, then chill.

Use to fill Fillo Tart Shells.

Top with a small scoop of Non-fat Frozen Vanilla Yogurt or Non-fat Frozen Vanilla Dessert, or Dream Whip.

[A] FRESH FRUIT WITH LIGHT RUSSIAN CREME
By Susan Stokes

Serves 10   **Serving Size =1 Cup**   **159 Calories**   **2 Fat Grams**

1 envelope	unflavored gelatin	1/2 cup	reduced fat sour cream
1/2 cup	water		(1 g. fat per tablespoon)
1 cup	2% milk	2 tsp.	vanilla
3/4 cup	fructose	7-1/2 cups	fresh fruit
1-1/2 cups	low-fat vanilla yogurt		(strawberries, peaches, raspberries, or nectarines)

In a medium saucepan sprinkle the gelatin over the water; allow to soften for about five minutes. Add milk, and fructose. With a rubber spatula stir over low heat, scraping granules from the side of the saucepan, until the gelatin and fructose are dissolved (mixture will be warm, not hot). Remove from heat. Stir vanilla into yogurt and sour cream; whisk into dissolved gelatin mixture.

Fill 10 small dessert bowls or 1 cup size punch cups (about 3/4 full) with washed and *well drained* fresh fruit pieces. Pour Russian Cream over fruit. Cover with plastic wrap and chill to set.

NOTES

FROZEN FANTASY
By Susan Stokes

Serves 16   **Serving Size = 1 1/2" Wedges   1 Calories**   **1 Fat Grams**

2 1/2 cups	fat-free pretzel crumbs (Nabisco's Mister Salty)	2 quarts	Fat Free Frozen Yogurt or Fat Free Frozen Dessert (try using 1 quart each of two different flavors)
4 Tbl.	brown sugar		
4 Tbl.	Promise Ultra margarine (4 FG per tablespoon)	11.5 oz.	jar Smucker's light hot fudge topping

Crush pretzels into coarse crumbs in food processor or blender. Set aside 3/4 cup crumbs. Stir sugar into remaining crumbs, add melted margarine and stir until very thoroughly combined. (This works great in a food processor!) Spray a 9 inch spring-form pan with vegetable oil cooking spray. Pat the crumbs evenly and firmly onto bottom and sides of pan. Bake at 350 degrees for 8 minutes. Cool. Soften (don't melt) frozen yogurt so it will be easy to handle. Spoon 1 quart of the frozen into the cooled crust. Spread carefully. Sprinkle with half of the reserved crumbs, and drizzle with half of the slightly warmed topping. Put into freezer for 10 or 15 minutes, then carefully spoon on and spread the remaining quart of frozen dessert. Sprinkle with remaining crumbs, and drizzle with remaining topping (warm slightly if necessary). Freeze until firm.

To Serve: Loosen sides by sliding a thin knife blade around between pan and crust. Carefully remove sides; use a large metal spatula to transfer dessert to a serving tray.

NOTES

FRUIT COCKTAIL CAKE
By Susan Stokes

Serves 18 **Serving Size = 2" x 3" Piece** **124 Calories** **1 Fat Gram**

Rich and very moist - hard to believe it has so little fat.

3/4 cup	fructose	1/4 cup	brown sugar, packed
1 cup	w.w. flour	1 1/2 tsp.	baking soda
1 cup	all purpose flour	1	egg plus 2 egg whites
1/4 tsp.	salt	16 oz. can	lite fruit cocktail

Topping

1/2 cup	fructose	1 1/2 Tbl.	margarine
4 tsp.	Butter Buds	1/2 tsp.	baking soda
1/2 cup	skim evaporated milk	1 tsp.	vanilla
1 Tbl.	honey		

Preheat oven to 350 degrees. Spray a 9 x 13 inch pan with cooking oil spray and dust with flour. In a large bowl, stir together the flour, sugar, salt, and soda.

*Drain juice from fruit cocktail; add to the dry ingredients along with the egg and whites. Beat until batter is smooth; stir in fruit. Pour batter into prepared pan and sprinkle brown sugar evenly on top. Bake for 30 to 35 minutes. Remove from oven when a toothpick comes out of the center clean; cool on a wire rack for 10 minutes. As soon as cake comes from oven, make topping. * Fruit cocktail can be whirled in blender if you don't like the texture of small pieces of fruit in the cake.

Note: You can substitute 2 more egg whites, and leave the whole egg out if you have cholesterol problems.

Topping

Put all ingredients except vanilla in a medium saucepan. Bring to a boil, (this will foam up), stirring constantly. Boil 6 to 8 minutes; (should be pale tan and slightly thick) add vanilla. Drizzle slowly and evenly over top of the cake ten minutes after it comes from the oven.

Serve with 1 tablespoon prepared Dream Whip on top.

NOTES

GINGERCAKE
By Susan Stokes

Serves 18   **Serving Size =2" x 3" Piece**   **135 Calories**   **2 Fat Grams**

Smells and tastes so good on a cold autumn or winter evening!

1/3 cup	fructose	1 1/3 cups	w.w. flour
3 Tbl.	butter or margarine	1 cups	all purpose flour
1/4 cup	applesauce	1 1/2 tsp.	baking soda
2	egg whites	1 tsp.	cinnamon
1/2 cup	honey	1 tsp.	ginger
1/2 cup	molasses	1/2 tsp.	cloves
1/2 tsp.	salt	1 cup	very hot water

Preheat oven to 350 degrees. Spray a 9 x 13 inch baking pan with vegetable oil cooking spray; dust with flour. Cream fructose and butter or margarine, add applesauce, egg whites, honey and molasses and beat until thick and smooth. Sift or stir dry ingredients together and add to creamed mixture. Add hot water and beat until smooth. Pour into prepared pan. Bake for 30 to 35 minutes, or until gingerbread tests done. Serve topped with Fruit Cocktail Sauce, or Lemon Sauce.

GINGER CRINKLES
By Susan Stokes

Makes 4 Dozen   **Serving Size = 2" Cookie**   **53 Calories**   **1 Fat Gram**

6 Tbl.	butter or margarine	1 cup	all purpose flour
1/2 cup	granulated sugar	1/2 tsp.	salt
I cup	brown sugar, firmly packed	2 tsp.	baking soda
2	egg whites	1 tsp.	cinnamon
1/4 cup	molasses	1/2 tsp.	ginger
1 cup	whole wheat flour	1/2 tsp.	cloves

In large bowl of electric mixer, beat margarine, brown sugar, egg white, and molasses (the mixture will look curdled.)   Sift or stir together all of the dry ingredients. Add to molasses mixture and mix until blended. Cover and chill dough (this is important - dough will be too sticky to handle if not well chilled.)   Form into balls (about 1 1/2 teaspoons dough) Roll in sugar to coat. Pre-heat oven to 375 degrees. Bake on an ungreased baking sheet for 8 to 10 minutes. Do not over bake, or they will lose their chewy texture. Store in an airtight container.

NOTES

GINGER LEMON PUDDING CAKE
By Susan Stokes

Serves 9   **Serving Size = 2 1/2" X 2 1/2"**   **153 Calories**   **2 Fat Grams**

A lemony sauce forms under the gingerbread like cake. Best served warm with.

1 cup	w.w. flour	1 tsp.	cinnamon
1/2 cup	all purpose flour	1/2 tsp.	ginger
1/3 cup	fructose	2/3 cup	water
4 tsp.	Butter Buds	1/4 cup	molasses
2 tsp.	baking powder	1 Tbl.	melted margarine
1/2 tsp.	baking soda	1/2 cup	fructose
1/2 tsp.	salt	1/4 cup	fresh lemon juice
		1 1/4 cup	boiling water

Preheat oven to 350 degrees. Spray an 8 x 8 inch square pan lightly with Bakers Joy, or lightly grease and flour. In a medium bowl, stir together flour, fructose, Butter Buds, baking powder, soda, salt, cinnamon, and ginger. Add the water, molasses, and butter, mix until well blended and pour into prepared pan. Combine remaining fructose, lemon juice, and boiling water. Pour carefully over the batter. Bake at 350 degrees 45 minutes. Cool 30 minutes before serving.

GINGER - PEAR CRISP
By Susan Stokes

Serves 6   **Serving Size = 1/6th of 9" Pie**   **149 Calories**   **2 Fat Grams**
(Not including yogurt)

This is a very simple, but nice dessert.

29 oz. can	lite pears drained; reserve 1/4 cup juice	1 Tbl.	honey
		4 tsp.	Wondra flour
1 Tbl.	lemon juice	1/2 tsp.	ginger

Topping

1/4 cup	quick oats
1/2 cup	gingersnap crumbs (10 Archway gingersnaps in blender)
1 Tbl.	honey
1 Tbl.	Promise Ultra margarine

Preheat oven to 350 degrees. Lightly spray a 9 inch pie plate with cooking oil spray. Arrange pear halves, cut side down, in pie plate. In a small bowl mix reserved pear juice, lemon juice, honey, flour, and ginger until blended and smooth. Pour over pears. Mix gingersnap cookie crumbs, honey, and margarine until mixture resembles coarse crumbs. Sprinkle over pears. Bake 20 minutes, or until juices are clear and bubbling. Serve warm with a small scoop of frozen vanilla yogurt if desired.

GINGER PUMPKIN MOUSSE
By Susan Stokes

Serves 12   **Serving Size = 3/4 Cup**   **141 Calories**   **1.5 Fat Grams**

Smooth, creamy, and spiced just right. I offer this as an alternative to pumpkin pie.

1 small pkg.	vanilla pudding & pie filling (cooked type)	1/2 tsp.	ginger
2 envelopes	Knox gelatin	1 tsp.	cinnamon
1 cup	skim milk	1/4 tsp.	cloves
1 1/2 cups	pumpkin	1 cup	skim evaporated milk
2/3 cup	fructose	1/2 tsp.	vanilla
1/2 tsp.	salt	1 envelope	Dream Whip, prepared according to pkg. directions
12	gingersnaps, coarsely chopped		

In a 4 quart saucepan, combine pudding mix and gelatin; gradually whisk in the skim milk. Bring mixture to a boil, whisking constantly; turn heat to low, and cook for 1 minute, remove from heat. Stir pumpkin, fructose, salt, all spices, skim evaporated milk, and vanilla together. Whisk pumpkin mixture into pudding. Put pan in a bowl of ice water; whisk mixture occasionally until it is cool and mounds slightly. Reserve 1/2 cup Dream Whip. Whisk the rest of the Dream Whip into the pumpkin mixture.

Fill 12 punch cups or dessert dishes 1/2 full of mousse. Reserve about 1/2 cup gingersnaps; sprinkle the rest on top of the mousse; divide remaining pumpkin mixture evenly over cookie pieces. Put cups on a tray, cover them with plastic wrap, and chill for 2 to 3 hours. Before serving, garnish with reserved Dream Whip and gingersnap pieces.

HOT FUDGE PUDDING CAKE
By Susan Stokes

Serves 9   **Serving Size = 2 1/2" Square**   **169 Calories**   **2 Fat Grams**
(Yogurt excluded)

The cake will rise to the top, with a chocolate sauce on the bottom. I think this is best served warm.

1 cup	flour	1/2 cup	skim milk
2/3 cup	fructose	1 tsp.	vanilla
2 Tbl.	cocoa	1/2 cup	brown sugar, packed
4 tsp.	Butter Buds	1/4 cup	additional cocoa
2 tsp.	baking powder	1 3/4 cups	hot water
1/4 tsp.	salt	1 1/2 tsp.	butter and margarine

Preheat oven to 350 degrees. Spray an 8 or 9 inch square pan with cooking spray. Stir together the flour, fructose, cocoa, Butter Buds, baking powder and salt. Stir in the milk, melted butter and vanilla. Pour into prepared pan. Stir brown sugar and cocoa together; sprinkle over batter. Pour hot water carefully over batter. Bake 45 minutes. While warm, spoon cake into dishes, spoon sauce over each serving. Serve with a scoop of non-fat frozen yogurt if desired.

LOIS' COMPOTE
By Susan Stokes

Serves 15	Serving Size = 3/4 Cup	145 Calories	Fat Grams = t

This is a beautiful and delicious dish to serve for Breakfast, Brunch, Dessert, or on a Buffet Table.

1 large can	pineapple chunks or slices	2 cans	mandarin orange
1 qt. or 1 large can	lite peach halves (quartered)		sections
1 qt. or 1 large can	lite pears (cut in half)	2 cups	water
1 pkg.	Strawberry Danish Dessert	1 lg. can	grapefruit sections

Drain all fruit, put in a large flat casserole dish. Prepare Danish Dessert in the microwave, or in a saucepan. Pour the sauce over fruit and cover with foil. Bake at 325 degrees for 45 minutes. Cool, stir gently several times while cooling. Refrigerate. Keeps about 5 days. **Tastes** better after 2 or 3 days.

LOIS' YUMMY POACHED APPLES
By Susan Stokes

Serves 10	Serving Size = 1 Apple	182 Calories	2 Fat Grams

This is one of the truly wonderful recipes from my mothers extensive collection.

10 medium	Jonathan apples	1/4 tsp.	red food coloring
2 cups	water	4 medium	bananas
1 cup	sugar	1 Tbl.	Dream Whip - per serving
1/3 cup	cinnamon red-hot candies	3 Tbl.	sliced almonds

Peel and core apples. Bring water, fructose, cinnamon candies and food coloring to a boil in a large enough pan to hold all of the apples in a single layer. Lay the whole apples in the boiling syrup. Simmer, turning and basing often, until apples are tender - about 30 minutes. Remove apples from the syrup, cover and chill. Just before serving, fill the center of the apple with a piece of banana, top with 1 tablespoon Dream Whip and 1 teaspoon sliced almonds.

NOTES

MATT'S FROZEN PUMPKIN PIE

By Susan Stokes

Whole Crust   **685 Calories**   **19 Fat Grams**

Cookie Crust:

3/4 cup	gingersnap crumbs (15 Archway cookies)
1/2 cup	graham cracker crumbs (Nabisco is a good low fat choice)
2 Tbl.	reduced fat margarine Promise Ultra (4 grams fat per Tbl.)
2 tsp.	water

Spray a 9 inch pie plate with vegetable cooking spray. Mix crumbs, melted margarine and water together very thoroughly. Pat evenly and firmly into pie plate. Bake at 350 degrees for 8 minutes. Cool before filling.

Filling:

Serves 10   **Serving Size = 1/10 of a 9" pie**   **171 Calories**   **2 Fat Grams**

1 quart	vanilla fat free frozen yogurt	1/2 tsp.	cinnamon
	or fat free frozen dessert	1/2 tsp.	ginger
1 cup	pumpkin	1/4 tsp.	nutmeg

Set frozen yogurt or dessert out at room temperature until slightly softened. Stir pumpkin and spices together; fold into softened frozen dessert. Turn into cooled crumb crust. Freeze until firm. Remove from freezer about 10 minutes before serving. Garnish each piece of pie with 1 tablespoon Dream Whip if desired.

MICHAEL'S EUROPEAN STYLE BAKED RICE PUDDING

By Susan Stokes

Serves 6   **Serving Size = 1/2 Cup**   **199 Calories**   **3 Fat Grams**

A wonderful old fashioned dessert!

Long slow baking five this pudding an almost caramel like taste. It goes together quickly, but does require lots of oven time.

3 cups	2% milk	1/2 tsp.	nutmeg
1 can	skim evaporated milk	5 Tbl.	raw rice (short grain works
1/4 tsp.	salt		great in this)
2/3 cup	fructose	2 tsp.	butter or margarine

Spray a 1 1/2 quart casserole dish with cooking oil spray. Put all of the ingredients into casserole, stir to blend. Bake at 300 degrees (no Higher) for 3 1/2 hours, stirring three times during the first hour of baking (every 20 minutes). Serve warm or cold.

MICRO-BAKED CARAMEL APPLES
By Susan Stokes

Serves 4   **Serving Size = 1/2 Apple**   **78 Calories**   **1 Fat Grams**

2 medium	baking apples
4 Tbl.	Kraft Caramel Topping (12.5 oz. squeeze bottle)
4 Tbl.	Dream Whip prepared with skim milk (optional)

Spray a 9 inch pie plate with cooking spray. Halve apples lengthwise; core. Drop 4 tablespoon size blobs of caramel sauce into the pie plate. Place apples, cut side down, over caramel sauce. Microwave, uncovered, at full power, for 3 to 4 minutes, until apples are tender. Place apples cut side up in small dessert dishes, stir caramel and apple juices together and spoon over cooked apple halves. Garnish with Dream Whip, if desired.

Note Cooking times:
1 apple takes 1 to 1-1/2 minutes
2 apples takes 3 to 4 minutes
4 apples takes 6 to 7-1/2 minutes
5 apples takes 8-1/2 to 10 minutes

DESSERTS

MILLIONAIRE CAKE
By Susan Stokes

2 Cakes   Serves 30   Serving Size = 2 1/2" x 3" Piece   151 Calories   2 Fat Grams

Tastes like a million! This recipe makes two large desserts.

Make a Pillsbury Lovin Lites white cake according to the recipe on the back of the box. Divide the batter evenly between two 9 x 13 inch pans. Bake at 350 degrees for 18 to 20 minutes. Cool on racks.

2 small pkg.	instant vanilla pudding mix (3.4 oz. each)
1 cup	plain non-fat yogurt
2 cups	skim milk

Beat on low speed of mixer for 1 or 2 minutes. Pour evenly over top of each cake.

Top with:
1. sliced bananas (3 large per cake)
2. well drained crushed pineapple (16 oz. can for each cake)
3. Dream whip (prepare 2 packages according to directions, and completely cover both cakes).

This dessert must be kept in the refrigerator.

*   **Well** drained fresh sliced strawberries or fresh raspberries are very good along with the banana slices.

Black Forest variation:

Serves 30   Serving Size = 2 1/2" x 3" Piece   145 Calories   2 Fat Grams

Use the recipe above as a guide, make layers using these ingredients:

1 pkg.	Pillsbury Lovin Lites Devils Food cake
2 small pkg.	instant vanilla pudding mix (3.4 oz. each)
2 cans	lite cherry pie filling (21 oz.) with 1/2 teaspoon almond extract and 1 teaspooon lemon juice stirred into each can.
1 Tbl. each	Smuckers Light Hot Fudge Topping - slightly warmed (drizzle over each piece when serving)

OAT AND RAISIN KISSES
By Susan Stokes

Serves 4 dozen   **Serving Size = 2 cookies**   **60 Calories**   **Fat Grams = t**

2	egg whites (from large eggs)	1-1/2 cups	rolled oats
1/2 tsp.	salt	1/2 cup	oat bran
1 tsp.	vanilla	1 tsp.	cinnamon
1/2 cup	brown sugar	2/3 cup	raisins
1/3 cup	granulated sugar		

Preheat oven to 350 degrees. Line baking sheets with foil and spray lightly with cooking spray (or use non-stick cookie sheet).

Beat egg whites and salt until stiff. Add vanilla and sugar and blend well. Fold in oats, cinnamon and raisins. Mix well. Drop by teaspoonfuls onto prepared baking sheet.

Bake 10 to 12 minutes. Cool 1 to 2 minutes before removing from baking sheets.

OLD FASHIONED "OLD FRUIT" CAKE
By Susan Stokes

Serves 20   **Serving Size = 2 1/4"x 2 1/2" Piece**   **200 Calories**   **2.5 Fat Grams**

This is a heavy, moist, spicy cake. It needs no frosting - keeps well.

2 1/4 cups	w.w. flour	1 tsp.	cloves
2 cups	all purpose flour	1 cup	raisins
1 1/3 cups	fructose	3 Tbl.	Canola oil (cold pressed)
1 tsp.	salt	1/3 cup	plain nonfat yogurt
1 tsp.	baking powder	1 qt.	fruit (apricots, plums or
4 tsp.	cinnamon		peaches are good)
2 tsp.	nutmeg	2 tsp.	soda

Preheat oven to 350 degrees. Spray a 9 x 13 inch pan with vegetable cooking spray; dust with flour. Put first 8 ingredients into a large bowl, stir together well; stir in raisins. Puree fruit in blender, add soda (it will quickly foam up). Pour pureed fruit, yogurt, and oil into dry ingredients. Mix well. Pour into prepared pan. Bake for 1 hour or until a toothpick comes out clean. Cool on a rack.

NOTES

DESSERTS

PEACH SHAKE
By Susan Stokes
Smooth, Delicious.

Serves 3	Serving Size = 1 Cup	364 Calories	0 Fat Grams

1 cup	unsweetened frozen sliced peaches
1	frozen banana
1 cups	Orchard Peach fruit juice (made from concentrate)
1 cup	vanilla nonfat frozen yogurt

Combine all ingredients in blender container. Cover and process until smooth. Serve immediately.

PINEAPPLE APRICOT COOKIES
By Susan Stokes

Serves 4 dozen	Serving Size = 2" Cookie	45 Calories	1 Fat Gram

Fruity and delicious!

4 Tbl.	butter	3/4 cup	drained crushed pineapple
1/4 cup	brown sugar, firmly packed	1 1/3 cups	w.w. flour
1/2 cup	fructose	2/3 cup	all purpose flour
2	egg whites	1 tsp.	baking powder
1 tsp.	vanilla	1/2 tsp.	baking soda
1/2 cup	dried apricots cut * into raisin size pieces (measure after cutting)	1/2 tsp.	salt

Beat together butter, brown sugar, fructose, egg whites, and vanilla together until very well mixed, stir in apricots and pineapple. Sift or stir dry ingredients together, and stir into pineapple mixture. Drop by spoonfuls about 2 inches apart on lightly greased cookie sheets. Bake at 375 degrees for 12 to 15 minutes, or until lightly browned.

* Use raisins as an alternative.

PINEAPPLE-BANANA SORBET
By Susan Stokes

Serves 8 small	Serving Size = 12 Cup	62 Calories	0 Fat Grams

1 small	ripe banana, cut into thick slices
20 oz. can	unsweetened pineapple chunks, drained, reserve juice
1/4 cup	skim evaporated milk
1/4 tsp. each	vanilla and coconut extract

Prepare 1/2 batch at a time if using a blender. Lay banana slices and pineapple chunks on a plastic wrap lined cookie sheet in a single layer. Freeze. When you are ready to serve sorbet, put banana pineapple, milk, vanilla and reserved juice in food processor or blender. Process about one minute, or until mixture is thick, smooth and creamy. Serve immediately.

DESSERTS

PUMPKIN CAKE ROLL
By Susan Stokes

| Serves 12 | Serving Size = 1/12th | 168 Calories | 3 Fat Grams |

2	eggs plus 2 egg whites	1 tsp.	baking powder
1 cup	granulated sugar	2 tsp.	cinnamon
2/3 cup	pumpkin	2 tsp.	cinnamon
1 teaspoon	lemon juice	1 tsp.	ginger
3/4 cup	flour	1/2 tsp.	nutmeg
2 Tbl.	cornstarch	1/2 tsp.	salt
1 qt.	fat free vanilla frozen yogurt, slightly softened	1/4 cup	finely chopped pecans or walnuts

Preheat oven to 375 degrees.

Lightly spray a 15x10x1 inch baking pan with vegetable cooking spray; line with wax paper, and spray with cooking spray again. Beat eggs, egg whites, and sugar on high speed of mixer for 10 minutes. Stir in pumpkin and lemon juice. Sift dry ingredients into egg/pumpkin mixture; fold gently to blend. Spread batter in prepared pan; sprinkle nuts evenly over top of batter.

Bake for 15 minutes. Cool in the pan on a wire rack for 10 minutes. Meanwhile, lay a thin kitchen towel on counter. Sift 1/4 cup powdered sugar evenly onto the towel. Invert cake onto towel. Peel off wax paper carefully. Roll up cake and towel from a narrow end of the cake. Cool completely on a rack.

Gently unroll cake. Spread frozene yogurt to within one inch of all edges. Reroll gently, starting at the same end as when cake was originally rolled. Cover with plastic wrap; freeze at least one hour.

When serving, slice with a serrated knife.

PUMPKIN COOKIES
By Susan Stokes

| Makes 4 dozen | Serving Size = 2" Cookie | 46 Calories | 1 Fat Gram |

Plump, soft, and not too sweet. Just right for the cookie jar!

1/2 cup	fructose		
1/4 cup	brown sugar, firmly packed	1 tsp.	baking powder
1 cup	pumpkin	1/2 tsp.	salt
4 Tbl.	butter or margarine	1/2 tsp.	cinnamon
1 tsp.	vanilla	1/2 tsp.	nutmeg
1/4 cup	applesauce or non-fat yogurt	1/4 tsp.	ginger
1 1/2 cups	w.w. flour	1 cup	plumped raisins (pour boiling water over - let stand 2 minutes - drain)
1 tsp.	baking soda		

In a large mixing bowl, stir together fructose, brown sugar, pumpkin, softened butter, vanilla, and applesauce. Sift or stir the dry ingredients together and add to the pumpkin mixture; mix with a wooden spoon until all ingredients are well blended. Stir in raisins. Drop by rounded teaspoonfuls onto lightly greased cookie sheets. Bake at 375 degrees for 13 or 14 minutes.

PUMPKIN CREAM PIE IN A COOKIE CRUST
By Susan Stokes

Serves 8   **Serving Size = 1/8th or 9" Pie**   **234 Calories**   **4 Fat Grams**

The gingersnap crust really enhances the creamy, lightly spiced filling. This has become a favorite at our house.

Cookie Crust
Entire Crust = 685 Calories   19 Fat Grams

3/4 cup	gingersnap crumbs		
	(15 Archway brand cookies)	2 Tbl.	soft light tub margarine
1/2 cup	graham cracker crumbs	2 tsp.	water

Spray a 9 inch pie plate with vegetable oil cooking spray. Mix all of the crust ingredients together very thoroughly; reserve 2 Tablespoons, and pat the rest evenly and firmly into pie plate. Bake at 350 degrees for 8 minutes, or Microwave on High 1 1/2 minutes; rotate, micro. 1 1/2 more minutes. Cool.

Pumpkin Cream Filling
Entire Filling = 1164 Calories   11 Fat Grams

1 1/2 cups	skim milk	1/4 tsp.	ginger
2 small pkgs.	instant vanilla pudding	1/8 tsp.	cloves
	mix (3.4 oz. size)	1 cup	prepared Dream Whip
1 cup	pumpkin		(reserve the rest for
1/2 tsp.	cinnamon		garnish)

Combine all filling ingredients in a narrow deep bowl. Beat at low speed with an electric mixer for 1 to 2 minutes. Pour into cooled cookie crust. Chill at least 4 hours - until set. Garnish with reserved Dream Whip and crumbs.

QUICK BERRY "ICE CREAM"
By Susan Stokes

Serves 10   **Serving Size = 1/2 Cup**   **155 Calories**   **Fat Grams = t**

1 1/2 cups	strawberry or raspberry or blackberry (all fruit jam)
2 1/2 cups	low-fat buttermilk or 2 cups plain non-fat yogurt plus 1/2 cup water

Stir buttermilk and jam together. Pour into container of Ice Cream Freezer, and freeze according to directions.

NOTES

QUICK FRUIT "PIE"
By Susan Stokes

Serves 6   **Serving Size = 1 Slice**   **99 Calories**   **Fat Gram = t**

Thickened fruit with a sweet and spicy crisp top. Easy and quick!

3 cups	fresh or frozen berries (one kind or a combination) or sliced apples		
1/3 cup	fructose	1 - 8 inch	flour tortilla (1 FG each)
2 Tbl.	flour (use a little less for apples)	1 tsp.	Promise Ultra margarine (Imperial Light is good)
1/8 tsp.	cinnamon	2 tsp.	fructose
2 tsp.	lemon juice	1/4 tsp.	cinnamon

Combine fruit, fructose, flour, cinnamon and lemon juice in a microwave safe 8 inch pie plate or cake pan; stir carefully, cover with wax paper. Microwave on high 2 1/2 minutes; stir, cover and micro. 2 1/2 more minutes, or until mixture boils and thickens. Uncover and set aside. Place flour tortilla on a paper towel; spread on soft margarine evenly; sprinkle with the fructose/cinnamon mixture. Micro. on high 1 1/2 minutes; rotate 1/4th of the way around, and micro. 1 more minute. Place tortilla on top of fruit. Serve warm, spooned into bowls and topped with non-fat frozen yogurt if desired. **Note**: This does not cut - you just crunch it through the tortilla with a serving spoon. You can use prepared apple or cherry pie filling if desired.

DESSERTS

QUICK PUDDING PARFAITS
By Susan Stokes

Serves 6   **Serving Size = 3/4 Cup**   **112 Calories**   **0 Fat Grams**

Tastes wonderful with any kind of fresh berry - also yummy with fresh peaches, nectarines, or kiwi.

1 cup	skim milk	1 small pkg.	instant vanilla pudding
8 oz. carton	non-fat lemon yogurt	2 - 3 cups	fresh fruit
1/4 - 1/2 tsp.	grated lemon peel		

Combine milk, yogurt, and pudding mix in a small bowl. Beat 2 minutes at low speed, or until mixture has slightly thickened. In 6 parfait glasses, make 2 alternate layers beginning with fruit. Chill until serving time. Garnish with 1 whole perfect berry or slice of fruit.

Variation: Substitute plain non-fat yogurt for the lemon yogurt. Add 1/2 teaspoon almond extract and 1 teaspoon lemon juice to a 21 ounces can of cherry pie filling. Alternate layers ending with pudding.

QUICK TO FIX CARAMEL APPLES
By Susan Stokes

Serves 2   **Serving Size = 1**   **72 Calories**   **0 Fat Grams**

What could be easier than this! Delicious for snacking or for dessert.

Slice an apple and use 2 tablespoons of Kraft Caramel Topping (in 12.5 oz. squeeze bottle) for dip.

READY IN A MINUTE FRUIT SORBET
By Susan Stokes

Serves 6-8   **Serving Size = 1/2 cup**   **98 Calories**   **0 Fat Grams**

5 - 6 cups	individually frozen pieces of fruit (strawberries, raspberries, blueberries, peaches, pineapple, banana)
2 Tbl.	fresh lemon juice
1 Tbl.	frozen orange juice concentrate
1/4 cup	fructose
3/4 - 1 cup	skim evaporated milk

Put all ingredients (start with less milk, and add more if needed) into Food Processor or Blender. If using a blender, process 1/2 of the recipe at a time. Blend for just a few minutes, until smooth and thick - this should have the consistency of soft serve ice cream. Spoon into dessert dishes, and serve immediately, or put into freezer until serving time. Process 1/2 recipe at a time if using a blender.

RICE PUDDING IN AN INSTANT
By Susan Stokes

Serves 6   **Serving Size = 2/3 Cup**   **250 Calories**   **1 Fat Gram**

3 1/2 oz.	instant vanilla pudding mix	1/2 cup	plumped raisins (pour the boiling water on, then drain)
1 cup	plain non-fat yogurt		
1 cup	skim milk	1/4 tsp.	pumpkin pie spice
3 cups	cooked brown or white rice	1/2 tsp.	vanilla

Prepare pudding mix with yogurt and milk. Stir in rice, raisins, and pumpkin pie spice. Spoon into dishes, refrigerate for 5 minutes.
This recipe is nice for breakfast, dessert or snack.
Note: Good for snack or breakfast.

NOTES

SKINNY DOUBLE DEVILS
By Susan Stokes

Serves 1   **207 Calories**   **2 Fat Grams**

Layer in a punch cup or stemmed dessert dish:

1. 1 piece   CHOCOLATE FIX^ or ZUCCHINI BROWNIES^
2. 1/4 cup   vanilla nonfat frozen yogurt
3. 1 Tbl.   Mrs. Richardson's Light Hot Fudge Topping (barely warmed)
4. 1 Tbl.   Dream Whip
5. 1/4   maraschino cherry

SODA CRACKER PIE
By Susan Stokes

Whole Shell   **986 Calories**   **4 Fat Grams**

No one will ever guess the secret ingredient!

3	large egg whites	14	soda crackers, 1/2 cup crushed
1 cup	sugar	1 tsp.	baking powder
1 tsp.	vanilla		
3 Tbl.	cocoa can be stirred into the cracker crumbs and baking powder if a chocolate shell is desired. (optional)		

Nuts are optional - just remember to add 9 grams of fat for every 2 Tablespoons of chopped nuts you add.

Preheat oven to 325 degrees. Spray a 9 inch pie plate with Bakers Joy, or grease bottom and sides. Beat egg whites until they begin to hold peaks. Add sugar gradually, beating constantly; beat in vanilla. Stir crushed cracker crumbs and baking powder together and fold into egg whites. Spread in pie plate. Bake until pale brown, about 20 minutes. Cool before filling. (The center sinks)

Vanilla Filling

Serves 8   **Serving Size = 1 Portion**   **210 Calories**   **1.3 Fat Grams**

1 envelope	Dream Whip	1/2 cup	plain non-fat yogurt
1 small pkg.	instant vanilla pudding mix	1 tsp.	vanilla
1 cup	skim milk		

(Well drained berries can be added as an option)

Lemon Filling

Serves 8   **Serving Size = 1 Portion**   **212 Calories**   **1.3 Fat Grams**

1 envelope	Dream Whip	1/2 cup	non-fat lemon yogurt
1 small pkg.	instant lemon pudding mix	1/2 tsp.	grated lemon peel
1 cup	skim milk		

Chocolate Filling

Serves 8   **Serving Size = 1 Portion**   **241 Calories**   **1.3 Fat Grams**

1 envelope	Dream Whip	1 1/2 cups	skim milk
1 small pkg.	chocolate instant pudding mix	1/3 cup	crushed peppermint candy (optional)

Combine Dream Whip, instant pudding, skim milk, yogurt and vanilla in bowl. Beat until stiff, about 8 minutes. Fill pie. Refrigerate at least 2 hours.

SPICY RAISIN PUFFS
By Susan Stokes

Serves 4 dozen　　**Serving Size = 2" Cookie**　　**72 Calories**　　**1 Fat Gram**

Made right in the saucepan!

These cookies are easy to make and wonderful to eat! They were a family favorite before I reduced the fat, and they still are!

1 1/2 cups	raisins	3/4 cup	fructose
1 cup	water	1/4 cup	brown sugar
1 pkg.	Butter Buds	4	egg whites
6 Tbl.	butter or margarine	2 cups	all purpose flour
1 tsp.	baking soda	1 cup	w.w. flour
1 tsp.	vanilla	1 tsp.	cinnamon
1/2 tsp.	salt	3 Tbl.	honey

Put raisins and water in a 4 quart saucepan. Bring to a boil, turn heat down, and simmer until water is gone (watch carefully when water is almost gone - don't scorch raisins.) Add Butter Buds, margarine, vanilla, salt, and honey soda to raisins; stir very well and set aside to cool for about 15 to 20 minutes. Add all remaining ingredients, and mix very well with a wooden spoon (be sure to get down into the bottom edges of your saucepan.) Drop rounded teaspoonfuls into a mixture of 1/3 cup sugar and 1/2 teaspoon cinnamon; roll in sugar mixture to coat. Place on cookie sheet that has been lined with baking parchment, or lightly sprayed with vegetable oil cooking spray. Bake at 350 degrees 12 to 14 minutes, or until light brown - do not over bake.

A

STRAWBERRY-BANANA-ORANGE SHAKE
By Susan Stokes

Serves 3　　**Serving Size = 1 1/4 Cup**　　**354 Calories**　　**1 Fat Gram**

4 Tbl.	orange juice concentrate	1	frozen banana
1 1/4 cups	skim milk	2 - 3	ice cubes
2 cups	frozen unsweetened whole strawberries		

Combine all ingredients in blender container (break banana into chunks). Cover and process until smooth. Serve immediately.

NOTES

STRAWBERRY SHORTCAKE
By Susan Stokes

Serves 1   **Serving Size = 1**   **296 Calories**   **0 - 2 Fat Grams**

1/12th	Angel Food Cake^ (9" cake)
1/3 cup	frozen vanilla yogurt (nonfat or low-fat)
1 cup	sweetened sliced strawberries

The only fat in this dessert will be in the yogurt.

TAPIOCA-FRUIT PARFAITS
By Susan Stokes

Serves 6   **Serving Size = 3/4 Cup**   **148 Calories**   **Fat Grams = t**

1 can	skim evaporated milk	1	egg white, slightly beaten
1 cup	skim milk	1 tsp.	vanilla
3 Tbl.	quick-cooking tapioca	1/4 tsp.	almond extract
3 Tbl.	fructose	dash	cinnamon
dash of	salt	20 oz. can	cherry fruit pie filling (lite)

Combine milks, tapioca, fructose, salt and egg white in a medium saucepan. Bring mixture to a boil over medium heat, stirring constantly. Remove from heat and stir in vanilla. Let stand for 20 minutes, stir, then cover and chill. Stir almond extract and cinnamon into cherry pie filling.

In 4 parfait glasses, alternate layers of tapioca pudding and cherry pie filling, ending with pie filling.

* Other fruit pie fillings taste great too.

THOUGHTS ON PIE
By Susan Stokes

It is fairly simple to reduce the fat in many recipes and still have a nice texture in the finished product. Some recipes should not be "fooled with", and I personally feel that pie crust is one of them. What to do? Here are a few hints.

1. Have pie occasionally - watch your portion size - enjoy it when you do eat it!
2. Make 4 crusts (tops or bottoms) out of a standard 3 crust recipe (49 FG per crust instead of 65) use 1, freeze 3.
3. Make single crust pies - put fruit filling in unlined pie plate top with a crust.
4. Use low or lower fat fillings. Do not dot with butter" as many recipes direct. Use skim evaporated milk in place of regular evaporated milk (you save 19 grams of fat per cup).
5. Think creatively about reducing fat in favorite fillings, and eat tiny portions of the ones that can't be reduced (Pecan comes to mind).

DESSERTS

TODD'S QUICK FRUIT COBBLER
By Susan Stokes

Serves 8   **Serving Size = 3/4**   **204 Calories**   **3 Fat Grams**
(Not including yogurt)

Preheat oven to 350 degrees. Lightly spray a shallow 2 quart baking dish with vegetable oil spray; put 2 Tablespoons butter or margarine in baking dish and put in the oven to melt.

1/2 cup	w.w. flour		
1/2 cup	flour	3/4 cup	skim milk
1 1/2 tsp.	baking powder	2 cans	16 oz. fruit (apple
1/4 tsp.	salt		slices, apricots, cherries,
2/3 cup	fructose		peaches, plums, pine-
apple)			

Stir dry ingredients together, add milk and whisk until batter is smooth. Pour batter over melted margarine; do not stir. Spoon fruit evenly over batter; pour juice over fruit and batter. Sprinkle with: 1/4 cup fructose mixed with 1/2 teaspoon cinnamon. Bake 45 to 50 minutes. Batter will rise to the top; test as for cake. Serve warm with a small scoop of frozen vanilla yogurt.

You can use 4 cups of fresh sliced fruit if you like.

TROPICAL FREEZE
By Susan Stokes

Makes 1 Quart   **Serving Size = 1/2 Cup**   **121 Calories**   **0 Fat Grams**

2 cups	plain non-fat Yoplait yogurt
2 medium	ripe bananas
12 oz. can	Chiquita Caribbean Splash frozen juice concentrate

Put all ingredients in blender. Blend until smooth. Pour into container of Ice Cream Freezer; freeze according to directions.

Other flavors of juice concentrate are good too! Be sure to try same of the other juice concentrates such as - (Chiquita Tropical Squeeze, Dole Pine-Passion-Banana.)

Yogurt with added gelatin freezes smoother than yougurt made without it. Read the labels.

TROPICAL SMOOTHIE BLENDER SHAKE
By Susan Stokes

Smooth, Delicious.

Serves 3   **Serving Size = 1 Cup**   **390 Calories**   **1 Fat Gram**

1 cup	vanilla nonfat frozen yogurt	1 large	frozen banana
1 cup	pineapple chunks with juice	5	ice cubes
3 Tbl.	Dole Pine-Orange Guava juice concentrate (undiluted)		

Combine all ingredients in blender (break banana into chunks). Cover and process until smooth. Serve immediately.

WHOLE WHEAT ANGEL FOOD CAKE
By Gloria Woodward

Serves 12   **Serving Size = 1 Slice**   **89 Calories**   **0 Fat Gram**

Angel food cake does not have shortening of any kind and no egg yolks so it is very low in fat. In additioin this recipe has been healtified in that half of the sugar has been cut from the original recipe. An excellent low fat, low sugar dessert. Egg whites should be seperated carefully so that no yolk gets in the whites of they will not become stiff. Also, all utensiols should be clean and free of any grease. Use a tube pan for baking but not a non-stick pan. Have eggs at room temperature and pre-measure all ingredients.

First pre-heat oven to 350 degrees. In medium bowl measure the following:

3/4 cup	freshly milled whole wheat flour
1/4 cup	cornstarch
1/3 cup	sugar

Stir until well blended. In a small bowl have measured:

1/3 cup	sugar

Make sure bowl and beaters are squeaky clean. Put salt, cream of tarter and egg whites into the large bowl of electric mixer.

1 tsp.	salt
1 1/2 tsp.	cream or tarter
2 cups	room temperature egg whites

Beat on high speed for about 2 minutes. They will be stiff but continue about 30- 45 seconds more as they will double in volume. Now turn your mixer down to medium and add the 1/3 cup sugar (1 tablespoon at a time), creating a meringue.

Add:

2 tsp.	flavoring (vanilla, coconut, almond, cherry, etc.)

Blend by pulsing the mixer a coupld of times..

Sprinkle flour mixture over the egg whites 1/3 at a time, and fold in each addition with a rubber spatula. After last addition scrape sides of bowl, lift and fold batter a couple more times. Pulse and blend in once more. Pile batter in ungreased tube pan and IMMEDIATELY place pan in pre-heated oven and bake for 40 minutes.

Angel Food cake is baked when it begins to pull away from sides of pan just slightly. Remove from oven and invert to cool. Never try to remove an Angel Food Cake from the pan until entirely cooled.

FRUIT TOPPING

10 oz. pkg.	frozen berries
1/2 cup	fructose or sugar
1 pkg.	berry kool-aid
1 rounded Tbl.	cornstarch

Thaw berries, reserve juice and add enough water to make 1 cup. Stir in sugar, Kool Aid and cornstarch. Bring to a boil stirring constantly. Cool, stir in berries. **Serve** on Cheesecake, cake, etc.

ZUCCHINI BROWNIES
By Susan Stokes

Serves 20   **Serving Size = 2 1/4" x 2 1/2"**   **104 Calories**   **2 Fat Grams**

Please don't let the thought of zucchini in brownies keep you from trying these - it is what keeps them moist!

2 cups	peeled, shredded zucchini	1 cup	w.w. flour
2 Tbl.	vegetable oil	1cups	all purpose flour
2 Tbl.	honey	1 tsp.	salt
2 tsp.	vanilla	1 1/2 tsp.	baking soda
1 cup	fructose	1/2 cup	cocoa
1/4 cup	plain non-fat yogurt		

Shred a little more zucchini than you need, and put in a colander to drain for 5 or 10 minutes. Preheat oven to 350 degrees. Spray a 9 x 13 inch pan with vegetable oil spray and dust with flour. Measure 2 cups of drained zucchini, combine with oil, honey, vanilla, fructose, and yogurt; stir to blend. In a large bowl, combine flour, salt, baking soda, and cocoa, stir together thoroughly. Add the liquid ingredients to the dry; mix well, and pour into prepared pan. Spread evenly in pan, bake for 30 to 35 minutes. Cool on a rack. These are nice plain, or dusted with powdered sugar. Cut into 24 pieces.

NOTES

DIPS - DRESSINGS - FILLINGS - SPREADS

DIPS - DRESSINGS
FILLINGS - SPREADS

SUGGESTIONS FOR DIPPERS
By Susan Stokes

All kinds of vegetables:

Celery Cucumbers
Green and Red Pepper Strips
Jicama (peel and cut in sticks or slices)
Radishes
Summer Squash
Broccoli
Carrots

Green Onions
Red Cabbage Wedges
Mushrooms
Snow Peas
Turnips
Cauliflower

Yams (slices or sticks - soak in 1 part lemon juice to 3 parts ice water in the refrigerator. Drain and put on relish plate when ready to serve).

Crackers and chips to make at home: see the Snack and Appetizer Section.

Breads and Crackers to buy:

Nabisco Snack Well Wheat Crackers
Bread Sticks (long thin imported ones - ie. Fattorie & Pandea brand)
Melba Toast
RyKrisp Crackers (plain has no fat)
Nabisco Mr. Phipps Pretzel Chips
Swedish Rye CrispBread (large and round, wrapped in blue paper)
Wasa, Kavli, and Finn Crisp are other brands of flat crisp breads that are available at the store

Just a final word on commercial crackers: READ the labels! Know what you are buying. Enriched is just another word for white.

BLENDED COTTAGE CHEESE - SOUR CREAM SUBSTITUTE
By Susan Stokes

Makes 1 Cup	Serving Size = 2 Tbl.	18 Calories	0 Fat Grams

This is my favorite substitute for sour cream in dips and dressings. I use yogurt and yogurt cheese a lot, but I do not care for them alone in veggie dips or dressings.

1 cup   nonfat cottage cheese
1 Tbl.   fresh lemon juice or buttermilk
1 Tbl.   nonfat yogurt

Blend in blender or food processor, scraping down several times, until absolutely smooth.

I like to make this at least several hours ahead and chill. It thickens, and the flavor mellows.

CALIFORNIA ONION DIP
By Susan Stokes

Makes 2 Cups   **Serving Size = 2 Tbl.**   **14 Calories**   **0 Fat Grams**

We like this just as much as the original made with sour cream.

2 cups	blended cottage cheese
1 envelope	Lipton Onion soup mix

Stir together, chill for several hours.

CHICKEN OR SHRIMP FILLING
By Susan Stokes

Serves 20   **Serving Size = 3**   **50 Calories**   **Fat Grams = t**

PINWHEEL FILLING VARIATION

8 oz.	YOGURT CHEESE^	1/4 cup	light sour cream
1/4 cup	Kraft Free nonfat mayonnaise	1/2 cup	minced onion
1 cup	finely chopped cooked	1/2 tsp.	lemon juice
	chicken breast meat **or**	1/4 cup	finely shredded carrot
1 can	shrimp - rinsed and well drained	1/4 cup	finely chopped celery

Stir all ingredients together. Follow instructions above to complete appetizers.

For the entire method of preparation refer to page 129 SAVORY SPINACH PINWHEELS^

CREAMY POPPY SEED DIP
By Susan Stokes

Serves 6   **Serving Size = 2 Tbl.**   **76 Calories**   **Fat Gram = t**

1/2 cup	VANILLA YOGURT CHEESE^	1 1/2 tsp.	poppy seeds
2 Tbl.	frozen pineapple juice	1 or 2 tsp.	white wine vinegar
	concentrate, thawed	1 Tbl.	honey

Combine all ingredients, stir well, serve as a dip with assorted fresh fruit. Or thin with a little skim milk, and drizzle over fruit salad.

EASY SALMON SPREAD
By Susan Stokes

Serves 12   **Serving Size = 2 Tbl.**   **43 Calories**   **1 Fat Grams**

8 oz.	fat free cream cheese product	to taste	hot pepper sauce
8 oz. can	salmon, drained and flaked	1/4 tsp.	dill weed
	fresh lemon juice to taste		

Stir all ingredients together. Chill for at least one hour to blend flavors. Serve with cucumber rounds, celery sticks, green pepper strip, melba toast, pita crisps, Ry Krisp.

DIPS - DRESSINGS
FILLINGS - SPREADS

FRUIT DIPS
By Susan Stokes

Here are some ideas for sauces to use as fruit dip or dressing for fruit salad (thinned if necessary)

CRANBERRY - ORANGE FRUIT DIP

Makes 1 1/2 Cups   **380 Calories**   **0 Fat Grams**

8 oz.	fat free cream cheese	1/4 tsp.	ginger
1/2 cup	CRANBERRY ORANGE SAUCE^		1/4 tsp. nutmeg

Stir together; chill.

YUMMY FRUIT DIP

Makes 1 1/2 Cups   **873 Calories**   **0 Fat Grams**

1/2 cup	skim milk	1 pkg.	instant vanilla pudding mix (3.4)
6 oz. can	frozen juice concentrate (try Dole blends)	1 cup	plain non - fat yogurt

Blend milk and pudding mix. Add frozen juice concentrate; stir until well blended. Fold in yogurt.

CREAMY SUMMER FRUIT DIP

Makes 2 3/4 Cups   **673 Calories**   **1 Fat Gram**

This is a lovely dressing for fruit salad too.

1 1/4 cups	skim milk	1 cup	slightly drained crushed pineapple
1/2 cup	plain non-fat yogurt		
3.4 oz. pkg.	instant vanilla or banana pudding mix		

Combine milk, yogurt, and pudding mix in a medium bowl. Beat until well blended. Stir in pineapple. Cover and refrigerate several hours.

LOW-FAT VEGGIE DIP
By Susan Stokes

Serves 16   **Serving Size = 2 Tbl.**   **21 Calories**   **0 Fat Grams**

1 1/2 cups	low-fat cottage cheese (1%)
6 Tbl.	plain non-fat yogurt
2 Tbl.	fresh lemon juice
1 pkg.	Hidden Valley Ranch Salad Dressing Mix

Put cottage cheese, yogurt and lemon juice into blender or food processor; blend until smooth. Pour into a bowl, whisk in salad dressing mix. Chill for several hours if possible.

Serve as a dip for veggies, or use as a baked potato topping. Thin as necessary to use as a salad dressing.

DIPS - DRESSINGS
FILLINGS - SPREADS

PINEAPPLE-PEPPER DIP
By Susan Stokes

Serves 24   **Serving size = 2 Tbl.**   **38 Calories**   **1 Fat Gram**

This dip is simple to make, but does require you to think ahead. Start at least 2 days before you want it.

3 cups	plain low-fat Dannon yogurt	2 Tbl.	minced parsley
8 oz.	crushed pineapple drained	2 packets	fructose
1/2 cup	light sour cream	3 - 4 drops	hot pepper sauce
as desired	finely grated lime peel	2 Tbl.	finely chopped green
1 cup	finely chopped red and green bell pepper		onion

Fresh vegetable dippers

Reserve 1/2 cup of yogurt (refrigerate)

Line a strainer with a light weight, white paper towel, or coffee filter. Set strainer over a bowl. Stir remaining 2-1/2 cups yogurt, pineapple, and fructose together; pour into lined strainer, cover with plastic wrap, and refrigerate for at least 24 hours. (The yogurt cheese should be as firm as cream cheese.) Put yogurt cheese into a bowl, stir in remaining ingredients. Chill at least one hour. Serve with fresh vegetable dippers.

PINEAPPLE PIE FILLING
By Susan Stokes

Serves 10   **Serving Size = 1/3 Cup**   **55 Calories**   **0 Fat Grams**

Stir together in a saucepan:

20 oz. can	crushed pineapple in juice	4 Tbl.	flour
1/3 cup	fresh lemon juice	4 Tbl.	cornstarch
3/4 cups	fructose	1/2 pkt.	Butter Buds (4 teaspoons)
1/2 tsp.	salt		

Pour crushed pineapple into a 4 cup measuring cup, add lemon juice, then fill to the 4 cup level with water. Stir dry ingredients together in a medium sauce pan. Add pineapple mixture to the dry ingredients in the saucepan. Cook until thick and bubbly. Lay a piece of plastic wrap or wax paper directly on the surface of the pie filling. Cool, then chill.

Use to fill Fillo Tart Shells.

Top with a small scoop of Non-fat Frozen Vanilla Yogurt or Non-fat Frozen Vanilla Dessert, or Dream Whip.

NOTES

POPPY CITRUS DIP
By Susan Stokes

Serves 8   **Serving size = 2 Tbl.**   **18 Calories**   **0 Fat Grams**

8 oz.   lemon non-fat yogurt
1 tsp.   poppy seed
1/2 tsp.   finely grated orange peel OR
                    lime peel OR lemon peel

   Combine all of the ingredients. Chill until ready to serve. **Serve**
with a variety of the seasons loveliest fresh fruits.
This recipe contains no fat.

SANDWICH SPREAD WITH CRACKED WHEAT
By Gloria Woodward

Serves 6   **Serving Size = 1/4 Cup**   **63 Calories**   **2 Fat Grams**

1 can   tuna (or any type ground or spreadable meat)
equal amount   cooked cracked wheat
to taste   pickle relish
 to taste   salad dressing

   Mix and spread on bread. The cooked grain takes on the flavor of
the meat. Great nutritional and budget stretcher.

SHRIMP DIP
By Susan Stokes

Makes 2 Cups   **Serving Size = 2 Tbl.**   **24 Calories**   **Fat Grams = t**

4 oz.   fat free cream cheese at room temperature
1 cup   blended cottage cheese
2 tsp.   fresh lemon juice
1 envelope   Italian salad Dressing mix. (dry)
1 can   shrimp, rinsed and drained

   Stir all ingredients together. This is thick enough to spread.

NOTES

SPINACH DIP
By Susan Stokes

Serves 18	Serving Size = 3 Tbl.	54 Calories	Fat Grams = t

16 oz.	VIVA non-fat cottage cheese	2 Tbl.	lemon juice
1/2 cup	Kraft non-fat mayonnaise	1/2 cup	light sour cream
1/2 cup	dry vegetable OR leek soup mix*	10 oz. pkg	frozen chopped
1/2 cup	fresh minced parsley		spinach, thawed, and
1/2 cup	chopped green onions		squeezed almost dry
1 small can	water chestnuts, drained	1 tsp.	dry Italian salad
	and chopped		dressing mix

Process cottage cheese and lemon juice in a blender or food processor until smooth, scraping sides of container several times. Scrape into a medium bowl. Add remaining ingredients; stir well. Cover and chill at least 3 hours. Serve with assorted low-fat crackers, melba toast, breadsticks etc., and raw vegetables.

* Pour dry soup mix into a bowl and stir it before measuring.

SWEET AND SOUR DRESSING
By Susan Stokes

Serves 8	Serving Size = 2 Tbl.	86 Calories	0 FG

Wonderful flavor when drizzled on a fresh fruit salad.

1/2 cup	orange or grapefruit juice	3 Tbl.	honey
1 tsp.	Worcestershire sauce	4 tsp.	pectin (used for jam)
2 Tbl.	white wine vinegar	1/8 tsp.	salt
2 Tbl.	catsup	1/2 tsp.	poppy seeds

Combine all ingredients in blender container (mini-jar if you have one). Blend until smooth. Chill at least an hour before dressing salad.

TEX-MEX FILLING
By Susan Stokes

Serves 20	Serving Size = 3	52 calories	1 Fat Grams

PINWHEEL FILLING VARIATION

1 1/2 cup	YOGURT CHEESE^	1/2 cup	light sour cream
1/2 cup	finely chopped green onions	1/4 tsp.	garlic powder
4 oz. can	chopped green chilies,	1/4 cup	finely chopped red
	well drained		bell peppers

Stir all ingredients together. Follow instructions on page 129 for SAVORY SPINACH PINWHEELS^. Serve with salsa if desired.

VEGETABLE AND HERB SPREAD
By Susan Stokes

Serves 10	Serving size = 2 Tbl.	38 Calories	Fat Gram = t

8 oz.	YOGURT CHEESE^	1/4 cup	light sour cream
1/4 cup	finely shredded carrot	1/4 cup	finely shredded radish
2 Tbl.	finely chopped green onion	1 Tbl.	fresh minced parsley
1/4 tsp.	dried basil leaf, crushed	1/4 tsp.	salt
1/8 tsp.	garlic powder	1/4 tsp.	worcestershire sauce

Stir all ingredients together in a small bowl. Cover and chill at least 2 hours for flavor to develop.

* **Spread** on whole wheat, low-fat crackers or bagels.

VIRGIN ISLAND DRESSING
By Susan Stokes

Serves 8	Serving size = 3 Tbl.	32 Calories	0 Fat Grams

1 cup	nonfat cottage cheese	1 Tbl.	lemon juice
1/2 cup	orange juice	1 Tbl.	brown sugar (packed)

In a blender at high speed, blend the cottage cheese, orange juice, lemon juice, brown sugar and salt until smooth.

NOTES

DIPS - DRESSINGS
FILLINGS - SPREADS

MAIN DISHES

MAIN DISHES

ANGELA'S SHEPHERD PIE

By Susan Stokes

Serves 6	Serving Size = 4 1/2" x 4 1/2"	304 Calories	4 Fat Grams

12 oz.	lean top round steak, trimmed of any fat & ground	5 med.	potatoes, peeled, lightly salted and cooked
1 medium	onion, chopped	1/2 cup	warm skim evaporated milk
1/2 tsp.	salt	1 pkt.	Butter Buds (1/2 oz.)
to taste	black pepper	2	egg whites, whisk until frothy
1-1/2 tsp.	worcestershire	to taste	salt and pepper
1 can	tomato soup	6	Kraft FREE singles (processed cheese), cut in half diagonally
2 cups	frozen corn, thawed, drained		
2 cups	cooked green beans, drain	as desired	paprika

Preheat oven to 350 degrees. Cook beef and onion in a large non-stick fry pan. Add seasonings, soup, green beans, and corn; stir gently to mix. Put into a shallow 3 quart casserole that has been sprayed with vegetable oil cooking spray. Mash potatoes; add milk, Butter Buds, egg whites and seasonings, whip until smooth. Spread mashed potatoes over meat and vegetables. Bake for 20 minutes; lay cheese triangles on top (they will overlap), sprinkle lightly with paprika and bake 5 to 10 minutes longer - until hot and bubbly.

MENU SUGGESTION

W	12 oz.
V	Tossed Green Salad
	No or Low Fat Salad Dressing
G	Whole Grain Roll or Bread
F	EASY BAKED APPLES^
P	ANGELA'S SHEPHERD PIE^ (optional)

NOTES

BAKED CHICKEN NUGGETS
By Susan Stokes

54 Pieces   **Serving Size = 9 Nuggets**   **177 Calories**   **3 Fat Grams**

Use these crunchy nuggets with dipping sauce as appetizers for twelve. Make them a meal for six by adding salad, potato, vegetables, and whole grain bread or rolls.

1 large	egg white	to taste	Taco Seasoning Mix
1-1/2 lbs.	boneless, skinless chicken breast, trimmed of fat, and cut into 1x2 inch pieces	1/3 cup	cornmeal
		2 tsp.	parsley flakes

Line a baking sheet with crumpled foil (small ridges help chicken get crunchy on both sides). Spray with cooking spray. Whisk white in a large bowl until foamy. Add chicken and mix to coat. Stir taco seasoning mix, cornmeal, and parsley together in a pie plate or shallow dish; add chicken pieces a few at a time. Turn each piece to coat with a thin layer of seasoning.

Arrange on prepared baking sheet in a single layer. Cover and refrigerate until ready to bake - up to 24 hours.

When you are ready to bake chicken, preheat oven to 475 degrees. Spray chicken pieces lightly with cooking spray. Bake 8 minutes or until chicken is opaque in the middle. Serve hot.

MENU SUGGESTION

W	12 oz.
V	OVEN FRIES^, CREAMY COLESLAW^
G	Whole Grain Roll or Bread
F	Lite Fruit Cocktail
P	BAKED CHICKEN NUGGETS^

VARIATIONS:

1. Replace Taco mix with a packet of Chili seasoning mix.
2. Mix 1/2 cup dry bread crumbs with 1/4 cup cornmeal, 1/2 teaspoon salt, and 1 teaspoon Creole, Italian, or Greek seasoning.

SAUCES FOR DIPPING

1. Combine 1/3 cup each plain nonfat yogurt and light sour cream (1 fat gram per tablespoon); stir in 2 finely chopped green onions.
   Wonderful to serve with Taco or Chili flavored nuggets.
2. Barbecue sauce
3. Sweet and sour sauce
4. Seafood sauce (my favorite is Skippers - found in refrigerated section, usually in meat department)
5. Cranberry Dipping Sauce - In a 2 cup glass measure combine the following: 4 ounces jellied cranberry sauce, 1/4 cup prepared BBQ sauce, 1/4 cup catsup, 1/2 teaspoon Worcestershire sauce and 1/2 teaspoon lemon juice. Whisk together; cover with plastic wrap, and cook on full power in microwave until bubbly.

MAIN DISHES

BAKED PORK TENDERLOIN
By Susan Stokes

Serves 4   **Serving Size = 3 oz.**   **141 Calories**   **4 Fat Grams**

1 lb.	Pork tenderloin, all visible fat removed, cut in 4 crosswise pieces
1/4 cup	plain non-fat yogurt
1/4 cup	SEASONED BREAD CRUMBS^

Heat oven to 350. Line a cookie sheet with foil. Spray with Pam. Spread yogurt on both sides of pork. Dip in crumbs to coat. Bake 40 minutes or until pork is tender when pierced and crumbs look dry and lightly browned.

MENU SUGGESTION

W	12 oz.
V	Baked Yams or Squash
	Tossed Salad
G	Whole grain Bread or Rolls
F	Fruit Cup
P	BAKED PORK TENDERLOIN^

BARBECUE TURKEY
By Susan Stokes

Serves 8   **Serving Size = 1/2 Cup Meat**   **209 Calories**   **2 Fat Grams**
1/3 Cup Sauce

1 can	French onion soup	1 Tbl.	Worcestershire sauce
1 can	Campbells Italian Tomato soup	1/4 tsp.	hot pepper sauce
2 Tbl.	cornstarch	2 pounds	boneless, skinless turkey breast, cut into strips. (Easier to cut if partially frozen)
2 large	clove garlic, minced		
1/4 cup	red wine vinegar		
1/3 Tbl.	honey		

Fry turkey in non-stick fry pan until lightly browned. Combine the rest of the ingredients. Pour over turkey. Cover and cook over low heat about 20 minutes. Serve over rice or pasta.

MENU SUGGESTION

W	12 oz.
V	Peas and Steamed Carrots
	Spinach and Alfalfa Sprout Salad
G	Whole Grain Rolls
F	FRESH FRUIT WITH LEMONY DIPPING SAUCE^
P	BARBECUE TURKEY^ Over Rice

NOTES

BEAN AND CHEESE ENCHILADAS
By Susan Stokes

Serves 8	Serving Size = 1		195 Calories	3 Fat Grams

8 corn	tortillas (softened in microwave)	1/2	green onion, sliced	
1 pkg.	Lawry's Enchilada Sauce Mix	4 oz. can	diced green chilies, drained	
8 oz.	tomato sauce	1/2 cup	nonfat cottage cheese	
1 Tbl.	chili powder		(drain if it has a lot of liquid)	
1/2 tsp.	ground cumin	4 oz.	Frigo Truly Lite mozzarella	
1/2 tsp.	garlic powder		cheese, shredded, divided	
15 oz. can	black or pinto beans, drained	1/2 cup	lite sour cream	

Make enchilada sauce according to package directions. Spray a shallow baking dish with Pam, spoon some sauce into the bottom of the dish. Slightly mash beans, stir in chili powder, cumin, garlic powder, 1/2 of the onion, and green chilies. Spoon 1/8 of this mixture down center of tortilla, stir 1/2 grated mozzerella into cottage cheese mixture, top with 3 tablespoon cottage cheese, mixture roll up, and put seam side down into prepared baking dish. When all of the enchiladas have been filled, pour remaining sauce over them. Sprinkle cheese on top. Bake at 350 degrees for about 20 minutes. Serve on shredded lettuce, with a tablespoon of sour cream and a sprinkle of green onion on top.

MENU SUGGESTION

W	12 oz.
V	included in enchiladas
G	TEX-MEX RICE^
F	Jicama sticks, green and red pepper strips
P	TURKEY ENCHILADAS^
D	PINEAPPLE BANANA SORBET^

NOTES

MAIN DISHES

BLACK BEANS AND RICE

By Susan Stokes

Serves 8 **Serving Size = 1 1/4 Cup** **298 Calories** **2 Fat Grams**

2 cups	dry black beans (turtle beans)	1 large	bay leaf
6 cups	water	2-1/2 tsp.	dried oregano, crumbled
2-1/2 cups	chicken broth	1-1/4 tsp.	salt
2 large	onions, chopped	1/4 - 1/2 tsp.	hot red pepper flakes
1 large	green pepper, chopped reserve 1/4 cup	16 oz.	can tomatoes, cut up save juice
1 large	red pepper, chopped	2 - 3 Tbl.	fresh lemon juice
3 ribs	celery, chopped	1/4 cup	green onion, sliced
2 large	cloves garlic, minced	1 cup	hot cooked brown rice*

Sort and rinse beans. Soak in 6 cups room temperature water overnight. (Or, quick soak by bringing beans and water to a boil. Reduce heat, simmer beans for 2 minutes. Remove from heat. Cover and let stand for 1 hour.) Drain beans and proceed with recipe.

In a large pan combine beans, broth, onion, green and red pepper, celery, garlic, bay leaf, oregano, salt and red pepper flakes. Bring to a boil on high heat; reduce heat. Simmer, covered for about 2 hours, or until beans are tender. Stir in un-drained tomatoes; simmer 15 more minutes. Discard bay leaf. Stir in lemon juice. Taste and adjust seasonings.

Ladle beans with liquid into 6 soup dishes or bowls. Spoon hot brown rice into the center of each dish; sprinkle with green onion and reserved red bell pepper.

* **Reserve** the juice

MENU SUGGESTION

W	12 oz.
V	Crisp Raw Vegetable Plate
G	Bread Sticks
F	Pudding with Fruit
P	BLACK BEANS AND RICE^

NOTES

BRANDON'S BEEF NOODLE STROGANOFF
By Susan Stokes

Serves 6	Serving Size = 1 1/4 Cup	294 Calories	4 Fat Grams

12 oz.	lean beef top round steak, completely trimmed of fat, and sliced thin (slicing is easier if beef is partially frozen)	1 can	undiluted condensed consomme
		1/4 cup	water
		1/2 tsp.	salt
		1/4 tsp.	pepper
1 medium	onion, chopped	8 oz	spiral macaroni
1 large	clove garlic, minced		(Rotini or Rotelle)
6 oz. can	mushrooms with juice **OR**	2 Tbl.	snipped parsley
2 cups	fresh sliced mushrooms	6 Tbl.	lite sour cream
3 Tbl.	lemon juice		(1 gram per Tbl.)

Saute beef strips, onion and garlic in a large non-stick fry pan, over medium high heat. Or spray regular skillet with Pam. When meat is lightly browned, stir in mushrooms with their juice, lemon juice, consomme, and pepper. Simmer for 5 minutes. Stir in macaroni. Cover and cook until noodles are tender, about 15 minutes, stir occasionally.

Top each serving with 1 tablespoon lite sour cream, sprinkle with 1 teaspoon parsley.

MENU SUGGESTION

W	12 oz.
V	Petite Peas and Steamed Carrots
	Tossed Salad
G	Whole grain Bread or Rolls
F	Fruit Cocktail - Lite Syrup
P	BRANDON'S BEEF NOODLE STROGANOFF^

NOTES

MAIN DISHES

BULGUR CHEESE BAKE
By Susan Stokes

Serves 8   **Serving Size = 3" x 2 1/2"**   **199 Calories**   **3 Fat Grams**

2 cups	water	4	egg whites
2 tsp.	granular bouillon	1/4 tsp.	pepper
	(beef or chicken)	1/2 cup	skim evaporated milk
1 cup	bulgur** OR 3 cups	6 slices	Kraft Free
	cooked brown rice		Singles(slivered)
thin coat	Nonfat cooking spray	2 oz.	parmesan cheese, grate fresh
1 large	onion, finely chopped	3 oz.	Frigo Truly Lite mozzarella, grated
2 cloves	garlic, minced	1 pkg.	chopped spinach (10 oz.),
16 oz. can	whole Italian plum		(frozen, thawed and well drained)
	tomatoes, drained,		
	and chopped		

Herbed Sauce: Mix 1 (15 oz.) can tomato sauce with l/2 teaspoon basil or Italian seasoning, stir and heat until warm. Preheat oven to 350 degrees.

Lightly spray a shallow 1-1/2 quart casserole dish with nonfat cooking spray. If using bulgur, bring water and bouillon to boiling in a medium sized saucepan. Add bulgur. Lower heat; simmer, uncovered, 15 minutes or until liquid is absorbed. Set pan aside. Spray medium sized skillet with nonfat cooking spray and heat skillet over a medium heat. Add onion and garlic to skillet; saute for 5 minutes. Stir in tomatoes and pepper; cook 5 minutes. Stir onion mixture into bulgur. Beat egg whites in a large bowl. Add all of the cheeses, milk, spinach, and the bulgur mixture, stir until well mixed. Pour into prepared casserole dish. Bake for 30 minutes, or until set in the center. Remove casserole to a heat proof surface and let stand 15 minutes before serving. Pass warmed herbed tomato sauce.

NOTE: To make individual casseroles, spray eight ramekins with cooking spray; divide mixture evenly among prepared dishes. Bake 20 minutes, or until set. Let stand 10 minutes. Run a metal spatula around edges to loosen. Unmold; serve in a pool of warm tomato sauce.

** **Find** Bulgur wheat in the bulk section or import aisle of the supermarket, Middle East markets, or Health Food stores.

MENU SUGGESTION

W	12 oz.
V	Tossed Salad
	No or Low Fat Salad Dressing
	Italian Green Beans
G	GARLIC CHEESE TOAST^
F	BROILED FRUIT OVER FROZEN VANILLA YOGURT^
P	BULGUR CHEESE BAKE^

MAIN DISHES

CALIFORNIA TACOS

By Susan Stokes

Serves 8	Serving Size = 1 Taco	Calories	Fat Grams
	TURKEY	458	5
	CHICKEN	460	6
	EYE OF ROUND	460	6

8 oz.	shredded poached turkey breast, chicken breast or 8 oz. left-over beef eye of round roast, diced.	1/2 cup 2 oz.	sliced green onions finely grated sharp Kraft Light Naturals cheese
1 pkg. 1/2 cup	taco seasoning mix water	3 oz.	Frigo Truly Light Mozzarella, grated
2 cans	black beans or kidney beans, rinsed and well drained	1 cup 1/2 cup	salsa or picante sauce light sour cream
4 cups	cooked brown rice	12	corn tortillas (see recipe for
10 oz.	package frozen corn (cooked)		CORN TORTILLA CHIPS^)
5 - 6	chopped tomatoes	1 head	shredded lettuce

Put chicken or beef into skillet with taco seasoning, water and beans. Simmer together for 15 minutes. Everyone makes their own California Tacos. First steamed brown rice, followed by meat-bean mixture, corn, lettuce, tomato, green onion, 3 tablesoons combined cheeses and salsa. Top with a tablespoon of light sour cream and some crushed "CORN TORTILLA CHIPS"

Optional: Instructions for Flour Tortilla Salad "Bowl" are with Crispy Dessert Shells.

MENU SUGGESTION

W	12 oz.
V	included in taco
G	brown rice
F	Peach halves with non-fat vanilla yogurt
P	CALIFORNIA TACOS^

NOTES

MAIN DISHES

CHICKEN BREASTS WITH CHIPPED TURKEY
By Heidi Neumarker

Serves 8	Serving Size = 1 Breast	296 Calories	8.6 Fat Grams
4 large	chicken breasts	1 cup	low-fat sour cream
2 1/2 oz.	chipped turkey	4 strips	turkey bacon (partially
1 can	cream of mushroom soup		fried)

Bone and skin chicken breasts. Cut in half, making 8 pieces. Wrap each piece with 1/2 strip of partially fried bacon. Line pyrex dish with chipped turkey. Mix sour cream and soup together. Arrange chicken breasts on top of chipped turkey. Pour cream and soup on top. Set in refrigerator overnight. Bake at 250 degrees uncovered for 3 hours.

Serve with brown rice seasoned with onion soup. also great for storing in freezer.

CHICKEN CORDON BLEU
By Susan Stokes

Serves 4	Serving Size = 4 slices ea.	218 Calories	6 Fat Grams
4	boneless, skinless chicken breast halves (4 oz. each)	1/4 cup / 1	parsley, finely minced / egg white
2 oz.	extra lean ham, slice thin	2 Tbl.	water
1 oz.	Kraft Light Naturals swiss cheese, grated	1/4 cup	SEASONED DRIED BREAD CRUMBS^
1/2 oz.	Frigo Truly Lite mozzarella cheese, grated	2 Tbl. / 1/8 tsp.	parmesan cheese / paprika

Preheat oven to 400 degrees. Line a baking pan with foil, lay a cooling rack in the pan, and spray with cooking spray. Pound chicken breast halves between two sheets of wax paper with a meat mallet or the edge of a heavy plate, until 1/8 inch thick and as even as possible. Lay 1/4 of the sliced ham on top of each piece of chicken. Top with 1/4 of the combined cheeses. Sprinkle with parsley. Starting at the short end, roll up, tucking in sides as you go to enclose ham and cheese. Secure ends with toothpicks. Whisk egg white and water together in a small bowl. Combine bread crumbs, Parmesan, and paprika on a piece of wax paper. Dip chicken into egg white, then roll in crumb mixture to coat. Arrange on prepared rack. Spray chicken rolls lightly with cooking spray. Bake, uncovered, for 25 minutes, or until chicken is no longer pink, and juices run clear when tested with a knife. Remove toothpicks before serving. While chicken is baking prepare the sauce.

1/2 cup	chicken broth	1 Tbl.	light sour cream
4 tsp.	Wondra flour	1-1/2 tsp.	Dijon-style mustard

Combine broth and flour in a small saucepan. Cook over medium high heat, stirring constantly, until mixture thickens and bubbles. Turn heat to low, cook 1 minute longer, stir in sour cream and mustard; keep warm, do not boil.

To serve: Cut each chicken roll in 4 equal slices. Spoon sauce over sliced chicken.

MENU SUGGESTION

W	12 oz.
V	Steamed Green Beans
G	STUFFED POTATOES^ and Whole Grain Roll
F	SPINACH-CITRUS SALAD^
P	CHICKEN CORDON BLEU^

MAIN DISHES

CHICKEN ROLL-UPS
By Jan Greenwell

Serves 16	Serving Size = 1	158 Calories	7 Fat Grams

8 oz.	firm YOGURT CHEESE^	3 Tbl.	onion, finely minced
1/2 tsp.	salt	2 ribs	celery, finely chopped
1/4 tsp.	pepper	2 cans	Pillsbury Crescent
3 cups	poached chicken or turkey		Rolls (8 oz.)
	breast, cut into small pieces	1 cup	dry bread crumbs plus
3/4 tsp.	poultry seasoning	1/2 cup	crushed corn flakes

Preheat oven to 375 degrees.   Mix all ingredients except last four, in a small bowl.   Separate rolls into triangles, and put about 2 tablespoon of the chicken mixture at the wide end of each roll.   Roll up and tuck ends under, press to seal. Stir crumbs and poultry seasoning together, spread on a plate.   Roll each bundle in the crumbs to coat, press crumbs into dough if they don't stick.   Place on a baking sheet. Bake 25 to 30 minutes or until golden brown.   Serve with or without gravy. (These freeze well)

Gravy ideas: 1. Seasoned, thickened chicken broth.
2. Pillsbury Chicken gravy mix (in yellow box)
3 . White Sauce: Part chicken broth, part skim milk, thickened with cornstarch or flour - add some McButter for a richer taste.   Season with salt, pepper, and a pinch of poultry seasoning.

MENU SUGGESTION

W	12 oz.
V	Asparagus, Large Tossed Salad
G	included in roll-ups
F	Fruit Cup
P	CHICKEN ROLL-UPS^

NOTES

73

CREAMED TUNA

By Susan Stokes

Serves 6	Serving Size = 3/4 Cup	160 Calories	2 Fat Grams

1/2 cup	onion, finely chopped	1/8 tsp.	pepper
8 oz.	fresh mushrooms, chopped	4 tsp.	Butter Buds (1/2 pkt.)
3 Tbl.	Wondra flour	3/4 cup	skim evaporated milk
1 can	condensed chicken broth (low sodium) (10 3/4 oz.)	1/4 cup	Kraft Free fat free mayonnaise
2 tsp.	lemon juice	2 (6 oz.)	water packed tuna**
1/2 tsp.	leaf tarragon, crumbled	2 Tbl.	fresh minced parsley, (or 1 tablespoon dry)

Cook onion in a large non-stick fry pan for about 2 minutes, add mushrooms, and cook another minute or two, until vegetables are barely tender. Stir flour into the broth; add to the vegetables in the pan along with the lemon juice, tarragon, pepper, Butter Buds, and frozen peas. Cook, stirring constantly, until thickened. Stir skim evaporated milk into fat free mayonnaise and add to thickened mixture. Add drained, flaked tuna, and parsley, stir gently. Heat through, but do not boil. Toast whole wheat bread and cut into triangles.

Try this over steamed grain, baked potato, or pasta.

MENU SUGGESTION

W	12 oz.
V	Mixed Greens with Red Bell Pepper with No or Low Fat Dressing Steamed Carrots
G	included in tuna
F	fresh strawberries, watermelon and peaches
P	CREAMED TUNA^ over Toast Points

** **Substitute** canned salmon, crab, shrimp, cooked chicken or turkey. To use raw chicken or turkey, cut into cubes and cook with onions until meat is opaque.

MAIN DISHES

74

CRISP OVEN "FRIED" FISH

By Susan Stokes

Serves 4 **Serving Size = 4 oz. Fillet** **135 - 185 Calories** **1 - 8 Fat Grams**

1/2 cup	fine dry bread crumbs from	1	egg white
3 slices	whole wheat bread	1 lb.	fresh white fish
2 T	cornmeal		fillets, or 1 pound
1/4 tsp.	salt		block of frozen
3/4 tsp.	paprika		fillets, thawed 15
1/4 tsp.	onion powder		minutes at room
1/4 tsp.	dried thyme Leaves		temperature; cut into
lightly	vegetable oil cooking spray		4 equal portions.

Heat oven to 450 degrees. Tear off a large sheet of foil, crumple the foil, then line a jelly roll pan with it. Spray with Pam. (The ridges in the foil will help keep the fish from getting soggy.) Mix all of the dry ingredients. Beat egg white with a fork until it is frothy. Dip fish into egg white, then into crumbs to coat both sides. Place on prepared pan, spray each piece of fish with cooking spray. Bake 8 to 10 minutes for fresh fillets, 18 to 20 for frozen fillets, or until fish is opaque in center.

Serve immediately because this does not hold well.

MENU SUGGESTION

W	12 oz.
V	Broccoli / Cauliflower / Carrots
G	Potatoes, Rice or Pasta
F	Pineapple Sherbet
P	CRISP OVEN "FRIED" FISH^

NOTES

MAIN DISHES

CRUNCHY BAKED CHICKEN

By Susan Stokes

Serves 8   **Serving Size = 1 Piece**   **173 Calories**   **3 Fat Grams**

Preheat oven to 350 degrees. Line a baking pan with foil, and put a cake cooling rack inside; spray rack and foil with cooking spray.

8	boneless,skinless chicken breasts, (about 4 oz. each)
1/2 pkg.	dry Italian salad dressing mix
1/2 cup	buttermilk
as desired	crushed corn flakes

Combine salad dressing mix and buttermilk. Spread crushed corn flakes on a piece of wax paper. Dip chicken in buttermilk mixture; coat in crumbs and lay on prepared rack. Bake 45 minutes to 1 hour, depending on the thickness of the chicken.

MENU SUGGESTION

W	12 oz.
V	WALDORF SALAD^
	Steamed Broccoli
G	Whole Grain Roll or Bread
F	Peaches
P	CRUNCHY BAKED CHICKEN^
	CHEESY POTATOES^

NOTES

MAIN DISHES

FAJITAS
By Susan Stokes

Serves 10   **Serving Size = 1 Fajita**   **195 Calories**   **2 Fat Grams**

Here in Utah, Lynn Wilson and Villa Victoria both make a flour tortilla that is low in fat (1 gram).

1 large	onion, slivered	1 pkg.	Lawry's Fajita mix
1 large	green pepper, cut into thin strips	1 medium	tomato, cut into thin
1	red pepper, cut into thin strips		wedges
16 oz.	boneless, skinless turkey or chicken	10	flour tortillas
	breast, cut into strips	to taste	fresh salsa
1/4 cup	water	1/2 cup	light sour cream

Heat a large non-stick fry pan over medium high heat. Stir fry onion, and peppers until they are crisp tender. Remove from skillet and set aside. Stir fry turkey breast strips, add Lawry's seasoning and 1/4 cup water, blend well. Bring to a boil; reduce heat and simmer about 5 minutes, stirring occasionally. Return vegetables to skillet, heat, add tomato - serve immediately with salsa and sour cream.

Add 1 can rinsed and drained black or pinto beans to TEX-MEX RICE^.

MENU SUGGESTION

W	12 oz.
V	Tossed Salad
G	TEX-MEX RICE AND BEANS^
F	Fresh Fruit
P	QUICK AND SPICY CHICKEN FAJITAS^

NOTES

MAIN DISHES

FILLO WRAPPED CHIMICHANGAS
By Susan Stokes

Makes 8   **Serving Size = 1 Chimichanga   178 Calories**   **3 Fat Grams**

You can find Fillo (also spelled Phyllo) in the frozen foods department. The box has very clear directions about proper thawing and handling of the sheets of dough. I have been having a great time experimenting with Fillo. Try using this method to make egg rolls.

CHIMICHANGAS

1 1/2 pounds	poached chicken breast, shredded (or cooked and shredded top round or eye of round)	1 tsp.	oregano, crushed
		1/3 cup	canned chopped green chilies
		1 tsp.	ground cumin
1 large	onion, finely chopped	1/3 cup	light sour cream
2 cloves	garlic, finely minced	1/3 cup	bottled taco sauce

Preheat oven to 350 degrees. Spray a large non-stick fry pan with cooking spray. Cook onion and garlic over medium heat until they are softened (add a tablespoon of water if they start to stick - stir often). Remove from heat and stir in remaining ingredients, taste and adjust seasonings. WORK QUICKLY. For each Chimichanga, lay 2 stacked sheets of Fillo on a clean flat surface with the long side at the edge of the work table nearest you. Spray with cooking spray. Fold left to right like a book. Give fillo a 1/4 turn so that the long side is nearest you once again. Place 1/3 cup filling two inches from the edge nearest you and spread into a small rectangle about 5" X 2". Fold both sides of the fillo toward the center, then carefully roll up to enclose the filling. Place on a baking sheet - working quickly to finish filling the baking sheet. Spray Chimichangas with cooking spray. Bake for 18 to 20 minutes or until golden brown.

Serve on a bed of thinly shredded lettuce and spinach leaves, topped with a dollop of light sour cream, seeded diced tomatoes, sliced green onions, and extra taco sauce.

Note: Try using the filling in the recipe for SAVORY TURKEY BUNDLES^ Wrap and bake as instructed above.

MENU SUGGESTION

W	12 oz.
V	Bed of shredded lettuce and spinach leaves, tomatoes, green onions & sauce WARM CALICO SALAD^
G	Whole Grain Roll
F	PINEAPPLE-BANANA SORBET^
P	FILLO WRAPPED CHIMICHANGAS^

MAIN DISHES

FRUITED TURKEY

By Susan Stokes

Serves 4	Serving Size = 1 Cup		218 Calories	2 Fat Grams

8 oz.	jellied cranberry sauce, (1/2 regular size can)	20 oz.	can pineapple chunks
		to taste	salt and pepper
1 Tbl.	honey	12 oz.	turkey breast, cut into
2 Tbl.	cornstarch		bite size chunks
1 Tbl.	soy sauce	1 medium	onion, cut in 1/2, sliced
3 Tbl.	seasoned rice vinegar	1 large	green pepper, chunked

In a medium bowl, stir cranberry sauce until smooth. Add honey, corn-starch, soy sauce, vinegar, and all of the juice from the can of pineapple. Stir and set aside. Brown turkey chunks in a large non-stick fry pan, or spray a regular fry pan with cooking spray. Add pineapple, onion, green pepper, and cranberry mixture. Bring to a boil, stirring constantly. Reduce heat and simmer for 15 to 20 minutes, stir occasionally.

Serve over rice, 4 grain mix, bulgur, couscous or pasta.

MENU SUGGESTION

W	12 oz.
V	Steamed carrots and snow peas
G	Whole Grain Roll
F	included in turkey
P	FRUITED TURKEY OVER RICE^

NOTES

MAIN DISHES

GREEN TOMATO RATATOUILLE
By Susan Stokes

Serves 8   **Serving Size = 1 1/4 Cup**   **130 Calories**   **2 Fat Grams**

This is a good way to use your end of the season garden produce. I like to make many batches and freeze them in meal size containers. Serve over any cooked grain, pasta, or potatoes with freshly grated Parmesan cheese.

1 Tbl.	olive oil	12 med. ripe tomatoes,***	
6 med.	green tomatoes,** cored and coarsely chopped		cored and coarsely chopped
3 med.	green bell peppers, coarsely chopped	1 - 1 1/2 tsp.	black pepper
		1/8 - 1/4 tsp.	crushed red pepper flakes - optional
3 large	onions, coarsely chopped		
4 cloves	garlic, finely chopped (large)	2 tsp.	dry basil leaf
5 small	zucchini, cut thick slices	1 1/2 tsp.	salt

Spray a large heavy kettle with vegetable oil cooking spray; add olive oil and heat over medium high heat. Add green tomatoes, green pepper, onion, and garlic. Saute 8 to 10 minutes or until vegetables are softened, stirring often to keep vegetables from sticking (if they do start to stick, add a tablespoon or so of water). Add remaining ingredients. Bring to a boil. Turn heat down, and simmer, stirring occasionally until much of the liquid has evaporated, and sauce has thickened, about an hour.

** **Eggplant** or extra red tomatoes can be substituted
*** **36 ounces** of canned tomatoes can be substituted

Note: nothing needs to have peel removed.

MENU SUGGESTION

W	12 oz.
V	RATATOUILLE^, carrots and celery sticks
G	Steamed Brown Rice, Whole Grain Rolls or Bread
F	Melon with PINEAPPLE BANANA SORBET^
P	Parmesan cheese

NOTES

80

HAWAIIAN SUNDAES
By Susan Stokes

Serves 8   **Serving Size = *1 /3 cup diced chicken**   **277 Calories**   **9 Fat Grams**
(mixed dark & light)

This is a complete meal.

2 2/3 cups poached chicken, cooled and cut into pieces	sliced green onions
chicken gravy	sliced red peppers
	sliced green peppers
4 cups steamed brown rice	pineapple chunks
sliced celery	mandarin orange sections
mung bean sprouts	sliced mushrooms
sliced water chestnuts	maraschino cherries

Use your nicely seasoned poaching liquid - defatted, and seasoned to taste with soy sauce; thickened with cornstarch for the chicken gravy.

Each person builds his own sundae. Start with brown rice, and layer on the other ingredients. Top with a cherry. Yum!!

*Serving size equals 1/2 cup cooked rice (110 cal.), 1/4 cup gravy (89 cal.) and 1 1/2 cup veggies and fruit (68 cal.)

MENU SUGGESTION

W	12 oz.
V	included in Sundaes
G	included in Sundaes
F	Fruity Frozen Yogurt
P	HAWAIIAN SUNDAES^

HONEY-MUSTARD CHICKEN
By Susan Stokes

Serves 4   **Serving Size = 1 Piece**   **157 Calories**   **3 Fat Grams**

4	boneless, skinless chicken breast halves, 4 oz. each	2 tsp.	pineapple juice concentrate
1 Tbl.	Dijon mustard	1/8 tsp.	garlic powder
1 Tbl.	honey	1/8 tsp.	onion powder

Preheat oven to 500 degrees. Tear off four 14x12 inch sheets of regular weight tin foil. Spray center of each sheet with cooking spray.
Stir honey, mustard, juice concentrate, garlic powder, and onion powder together. Lay each chicken breast half on a sheet of tin foil. Make 3 diagonal slashes, 1/4 inch deep, about 1 inch apart on the top of each piece of chicken. Drizzle 2 teaspoons honey-mustard mixture over chicken.

Fold foil to make tightly sealed packets. Arrange packets on a baking sheet. Bake about 10 - 12 minutes.

MENU SUGGESTION

W	12 oz.
V	Tossed Mixed Greens with No or Low Fat Dressing
	Steamed Broccoli
G	CRUNCHY 4 GRAIN MIX^
F	Pears In Lite Sauce
P	HONEY-MUSTARD CHICKEN^

INDIVIDUAL BREAKFAST CUPS

By Susan Stokes

Makes 12	Serving Size = 1 cup	119 Calories	2 Fat Gram

4 cups	cooked* brown rice, 4 grain mix, or bulgur	1/3 cup	skim milk
2 oz.	Kraft Light Naturals sharp cheddar cheese, shredded	2 larges	egg
2 oz.	Frigo Truly Lite mozzarella cheese, shredded	2 larges	egg whites
		1/4 tsp.	salt
		1/4 - 1/2 tsp.	pepper

> egg / egg whites — or 4 Egg Beaters

Preheat oven to 400 degrees. Spray a 12 cup muffin tin with cooking spray. Whisk egg, egg whites, salt, pepper and milk together in a large bowl. Combine cheeses and cooked grain. Stir to combine. Divide mixture evenly into the prepared muffin cups. Sprinkle with paprika if desired. Bake for 15 to 18 minutes or until set.

Variation: Spray a small non-stick fry pan with cooking spray. Saute until barely tender, 3 tablespoons each, finely chopped red bell pepper and sliced green onion. Add along with 1 can (4 oz.) drained diced green chiles, and 1/4 to 1/2 teaspoon ground cumin. Serve with Salsa.

Individual Breakfast Cups can be frozen. To reheat, microwave each cup for 1 minute on full power.

* **I like** to cook extra rice at dinner time, then I can put this together quickly in the morning.

MENU SUGGESTION

W	12 oz.	
V	V-8 juice	
F	Fresh Fruit	
G	Whole Grain Toast	
P	INDIVIDUAL BREAKFAST CUP^	

NOTES

82

ITALIAN CHICKEN

By Susan Stokes

Serves 6	Serving Size =	1 Piece	Calories	Fat Grams
		1/2 breast	146	3
		1 drumstick	81	2.5
		1 thigh	113	5.7

2 lbs.	chicken, skin and all visible fat removed
6 Tbl.	Wishbone Lite Italian Salad Dressing
2 Tbl.	fresh lemon juice
1 tsp.	instant chicken bouillon
1/8 tsp.	pepper
1/2 tsp.	Italian Seasoning, crushed

Lay chicken in a shallow pan. Combine the rest of the ingredients and pour over the chicken. Cover tightly with foil. Bake at 350 degrees for 1 1/2 hours. Serve with pasta, rice or potatoes. The juices are delicious over any of these. (Be sure to remove any fat from the top of the juices before serving.)

MENU SUGGESTION

W	12 oz.
V	Green Beans, Tossed Salad
G	Pasta
	Whole grain Bread or Rolls
F	Fresh Fruit
P	ITALIAN CHICKEN^

NOTES

MAIN DISHES

LEMON CHICKEN
By Susan Stokes

Serves 1   **Serving Size = 1 piece**   **140 Calories**   **3 Fat Grams**

For each serving, you will need:

12 inch	square of aluminum foil	1	thin slice of lemon
4 oz.	skinned, boned chicken breast	1/4 tsp.	dried tarragon leaves
1 Tbl.	fresh lemon juice	1/4 tsp.	parsley flakes
1 tsp.	chicken bouillon granules	to taste	garlic pepper

Preheat oven to 500 degrees. Place each chicken breast on a square of foil. Gather foil up a bit so the lemon juice won't run out. Pour lemon juice over chicken, sprinkle tarragon, parsley, lemon, bouillon and pepper over meat, lay lemon slice on top. Seal foil well. Place foil packets on a jelly roll pan, bake for 10 to 12 minutes.

MENU SUGGESTION

W	12 oz.
V	Steamed Spinach
	Carrot Raisin Salad
G	Baked Potato
F	Fruit Sorbet
P	LEMON CHICKEN^

LEMON-LIME POACHED CHICKEN
By Susan Stokes

Serves 4   **Serving Size = 1 piece**   **150 Calories**   **3 Fat Grams**

4 (4 oz.)	boneless, skinless chicken breast halves	1Tbl. (round)	Dijon mustard
		2 tsp.	fresh lime juice
1/2 cup	chicken broth - low sodium	1/4 - 1/2 tsp.	finely grated lemon
3 Tbl.	fresh lemon juice		or lime peel
2 Tbl.	low-sodium soy sauce	1/4 tsp.	onion powder

Place chicken in a large zip-lock bag. Combine remaining ingredients; pour into bag and zip closed. Lay bag in a shallow dish, refrigerate several hours; turn once or twice. Drain marinade into a large skillet. Bring to a boil; add chicken and return to a boil. Cover and simmer 10 minutes, or until chicken is opaque, and juices run clear. Transfer chicken to the center of a large serving platter, keep warm. Cook marinade over high heat 2 or 3 minutes or until it is reduced by about half.

To serve: Surround chicken with drained pasta, drizzle reduced juices over all (strong flavor, a little goes a long way).

MENU SUGGESTION

W	12 oz.
V	Steamed Broccoli/Cauliflower/Carrot
G	Pasta
	Whole Grain Roll
F	Sliced Honeydew Melon
P	LEMON-LIME POACHED CHICKEN^

MAIN DISHES

MICRO-BAKED FISH
By Susan Stokes

Serves 4	Serving Size = 1 Piece	149 Calories	3 Fat Grams

1 lb.	white fish fillets, (Halibut, Hoki, Cod, Sole)	1/4 tsp.	freshly ground pepper
1/4 cup	plain non-fat yogurt	1/3 cup	dried bread crumbs
1 tsp.	Dijon style mustard	1 tsp.	parsley flakes
1/4 tsp.	thyme	1/2 tsp.	paprika

Cut fish into four equal pieces. Combine yogurt, mustard, thyme, and pepper in a small bowl. Combine bread crumbs, parsley flakes, and paprika.
Spread yogurt mixture on both sides of fish fillets. Place fillets on a microwave bacon rack that has been sprayed with cooking spray. Sprinkle crumb mixture evenly over fish.

Microwave on full power 4 to 4-1/2 minutes.

MENU SUGGESTION

W	12 oz.
V	Steamed Broccoli/Cauliflower/Carrots
G	DIRTY BROWN RICE^
	Whole Grain Roll
F	Cantalope
P	MICRO-BAKED FISH^

OVEN-BARBECUED CHICKEN
By Susan Stokes

Serves 12	Serving Size = 1 Piece	166 Calories	3 Fat Grams

3 lbs.	boneless skinless chicken breast
1 cup	Hunt's Barbecue Sauce - or your favorite brand,

Pre-heat oven to 375 degrees. Line a 9x13 inch pan with foil. Lay chicken in pan in a single layer. Bake, uncovered for 30 minutes.
Remove from oven and spoon off accumulated juices. **Pour** barbecue sauce over chicken pieces; return to oven for 15 minutes. Turn each piece of chicken over and spoon barbecue sauce on top. Bake 15 minutes longer.

MENU SUGGESTION

W	12 oz.
V	Baked Potato and Crisp Rainbow Salad
G	Whole Grain Roll or Bread
F	Sliced Oranges
P	OVEN-BARBECUED CHICKEN^

PIZZA STYLE SPAGHETTI
By Susan Stokes

Serves 6	Serving Size = 1 Wedge	179Calories	3 Fat Grams

8 oz.	uncooked spaghetti	1/3 cup	freshly grated parmesan
2	egg whites plus 1/4 cup skim milk (whisked together)	1/4 cup	finely chopped onion

Sauce:

2 cans	tomato sauce (8 oz.)
1 tsp.	Basil leaf
1 tsp.	oregano
1/2 tsp.	Garlic powder

Toppings:

3 oz.	shredded Frigo Truly Light Mozzarella	1/2 cup	small broccoli flowerettes
		2 Tbl.	minced parsley
2 oz.	diced extra lean ham	1/2 cup	finely slivered onion
1 cup	sliced mushrooms pineapple (optional)	1/2 cup	slivered green pepper any other no-fat ingredient

Cook spaghetti; drain, stir in milk mixture, onion, and cheese. Spray a 12 or 14 inch pizza pan with vegetable oil spray. Spread the spaghetti mixture on the pan evenly. Bake at 350 degrees for 30 minutes, or until firm when touched. Combine sauce ingredients, spoon sauce onto crust, spreading evenly to outer edges. Sprinkle on toppings and top with shredded mozzarella. Return to oven for 12 to 15 minutes. Cut into wedges to serve.

MENU SUGGESTION

W	12 oz.
V	Carrot and Celery Sticks
G	Whole-grain Bread or Rolls
F	Fresh Fruit
P	PIZZA STYLE SPAGHETTI^

POT ROASTED EYE OF ROUND
By Susan Stokes

Serves 12	Serving Size = 3 oz.	141 Calories	4 Fat Grams

Cut all visible fat from a 3 pound eye of round roast. Spray heavy fry pan with vegetable oil cooking spray and sear meat on all sides. Sprinkle a package of dry onion soup mix on top of meat or season to taste. Sprinkle black pepper as desired. Add 1 cup of beef broth (made with instant bouillon granules) or water to the fry pan, cover and simmer for about 3 hours. - This roast slices very nicely, and is moist and tender - Remove any fat from drippings (I had very little) and thicken for brown gravy.
Gravy - 5 calories, no fat per 2 tablespoons.

MENU SUGGESTION

W	12 oz.
V	Broccoli/Cauliflower/Carrots
	Spinach, Beet and Orange Salad with Sweet & Sour Dressing
G	Mashed Potatoes and Brown Gravy
	Whole grain Rolls
F	FRESH FRUIT WITH LIGHT RUSSIAN CREME^
P	POT ROASTED EYE OF ROUND^

MAIN DISHES

QUICK AND SPICY CHICKEN FAJITAS
By Susan Stokes

Serves 10	Serving Size = 1		190 Calories	3 Fat Grams

16 oz.	boneless, skinless chicken breast, cut into strips	1 medium	red bell pepper	
		2	cloves garlic, minced	
1 large	onion, thinly sliced	10	flour tortillas	
1 medium	green pepper, sliced	1/2 cup	lite sour cream	

Sauce:

1 tsp.	chili powder	1/4 tsp.	salt	
1/2 tsp.	pepper	1 tsp.	corn starch	
1/2 tsp.	cumin	1 Tbl.	lime juice	
		1/3 cup	salsa or picante sauce	

In a large non-stick fry pan, stir fry chicken strips, onion, green pepper and garlic about 5 minutes, or until chicken is opaque. Mix sauce ingredients together, pour over chicken, cook and stir about 3 minutes, or until everything is hot. Warm the tortillas, serve Fajitas with light sour cream and extra salsa if desired.

MENU SUGGESTION

W	12 oz.
V	JICAMA-CARROT SLAW IN PEPPER RINGS^
G	HOMEMADE CORN CHIPS AND SALSA^
F	READY IN A MINUTE FRUIT SORBET^
P	QUICK AND SPICY CHICKEN FAJITAS^

RYAN'S FAVORITE FISH DINNER IN FOIL
Easy, No Mess!
By Susan Stokes

Serves 4	Serving Size = 1 Packet		150 - 200 Calories	1 - 8 Fat Grams

1 lb.	frozen fish fillets (individual pieces, not a block)	2 medium	potatoes, scrubbed and sliced into 1/4 inch slices	
1/4 tsp.	dried dill weed	2 medium	carrots, peeled and sliced into thin slices	
2 Tbl.	fresh lemon juice			
4 tsp.	Butter Buds	1 cup	broccoli flowerettes (small)	
1 small	onion, sliced in thin slices	to taste	salt and lemon pepper	

Pre-heat oven to 500 degrees. Place each frozen fish fillet in the center of a 12 x 18 inch piece of foil. Measure the thinckness of the fish. Combine lemon juice and dill weed, drizzle over fillets. Divide onion slices, potato slices, carrot slices and broccoli evenly over the four fish fillets. Sprinkle lightly with salt and lemon pepper. Seal each packet tightly. Place on a baking sheet. Bake for 10 minutes for every inch of thickness of fish.

Variation: Stir together 1/4 cup orange juice, 1 tablespoon white wine vinegar, and 1 tablespoon soy sauce. Drizzle over 4 fish fillets as in above recipe. Arrange the following vegetables on top of each fillet in three separate piles: 1/4 cup chopped broccoli, 1/4 cup slender cut carrot sticks, 1/4 cup slender cut zucchini sticks. Seal each packet tightly. Place on a baking sheet. Bake at 500 degrees for 10 minutes per inch of thickness.

Serve with steamed brown rice.

MAIN DISHES

SAVORY TURKEY BUNDLES

By Susan Stokes

Serves 8	Serving Size = 1 Bundle	154 Calories	3 Fat Grams

12 oz.	poached turkey breast (or left-over roast turkey breast), coarsely chopped	1 oz. (1/3 c) 1/4 tsp. 1/4 tsp.	Parmesan cheese salt pepper
2 cups	green onions, slice thin	1/2 tsp.	garlic powder
10 oz. pkg.	frozen chopped spinach, thawed and squeezed almost dry	1/4 tsp. 1/4 tsp.	dried oregano, crushed nutmeg
1 cup	fat free cottage cheese	1 tsp.	lemon juice
6 slices	Borden Fat Free Swiss Cheese, singles, slivered	8	egg roll wrappers

Preheat oven to 350 degrees. Spray eight 10 oz. custard cups or ramekins with Pam. In a large mixing bowl combine all ingredients except egg roll wrappers. Mix thoroughly. Line each prepared cup with an egg roll wrapper. Divide turkey mixture evenly among the 8 dishes. Fold the ends of each wrapper over the top of the turkey mixture to make a bundle. Spray tops of bundles with Pam. Bake for 22 to 25 minutes or until tops are golden brown.

Serve in cups or loosen bundles with a knife and remove.

MENU SUGGESTION

W	12 oz.
V	Steamed Carrots
G	STEAMED BROWN RICE OR BULGUR^
F	Fruit Cup
P	SAVORY TURKEY BUNDLES^

NOTES

MAIN DISHES

SIMPLY WONDERFUL ORANGE ROUGHY
By Susan Stokes

| **Serves 1** | **Serving Size = 1 Packet** | **97 Calories** | **1 Fat Gram** |

This method workes beautifully with other types of fish fillets. You can also add (match-stick size) cut-up carrots, zucchini or small broccoli flowerettes to the packet.

For each serving you will need:

4 oz.	orange roughy fillet		to taste	Molly McButter
2 slices	onion		3 thin slices	lemon
dash	salt		to taste	lemon pepper

Pre-heat oven to 500 degrees. Line a heavy baking pan with tin foil. Lay a piece of foil on the counter, place fish fillet in center of the foil, fold any thin pieces under so that fillet is as evenly thick as possible. Sprinkle both sides of fish quite generously with Molly McButter and lemon pepper. Sprinkle on just a dash of salt. Lay rings of onion and lemon slices on top of fish. Measure thickness of fish. Wrap with foil, making sure that all edges are sealed tightly. Place lined baking pan in the oven for 3 minutes to get good and hot. Put packet of fish seam side down on pan; turn over midway through cooking period. Fish should cook 10 minutes for every inch of thickness.

MENU SUGGESTION

W	12 oz.
V	Steamed Spinach
G	CRUNCHY 4 GRAIN MIX^
	Whole Grain Roll
F	Fruit Cocktail Cup
P	SIMPLY WONDERFUL ORANGE ROUGHY^

NOTES

SKILLET PASTA
By Susan Stokes

Serves 4 **Serving size = 1 Cup** **323 Calories** **5 Fat Grams**

1 large	onion, chopped	1/4 tsp.	salt
1 large	garlic bud, minced	Dashes	hot red-pepper sauce
2 tsp.	olive oil	3/4 cup	hot water
1/2 lb.	uncooked vermicelli	1 tsp.	basil
3-1/2 cups	canned tomatoes	1/4 cup	fresh or 2 Tbl. dry parsley
	and juice (28 oz.)	4 Tbl.	parmesan cheese, freshly grated
1 can	Campbell's Italian Tomato Soup		

In a large skillet, saute onion and garlic in olive oil until tender. Break pasta in half and sprinkle into skillet. Spoon tomatoes over pasta. Stir together juice from tomatoes, tomato soup, salt, and desired amount of pepper sauce. Pour over pasta, bring to a boil and cover skillet. Boil gently for 2 minutes. Add water and basil; stir with a fork to prevent pasta from sticking together. Cook, covered, stirring occasionally, about 15 minutes or until pasta is cooked. Taste and adjust seasonings. Stir in parsley.

Serve pasta topped with 1 tablespoon grated Parmesan cheese per serving.

MENU SUGGESTION

W	12 oz.
V	Tossed Salad with No or Low Fat Dressing
	Steamed Cauliflower and Petite Peas
G	GARLIC CHEESE TOAST^, ONE POT PASTA^
F	Fruit with Lemon Yogurt Sauce
P	Included in Pasta

NOTES

SOFT SHELL TACOS

By Susan Stokes

Serves 8	Serving Size = 3 Tacos	Calories	Fat Grams
	3 TURKEY	387	6
	3 CHICKEN	389	6
	3 BEEF	390	7

8 oz.	cook & shred turkey or chicken breast, or left over eye-of round roast, shredded	24	corn tortillas
		5 medium	tomatoes, diced
		1/2 head	lettuce, shredded
1 medium	onion, chopped	2 oz.	finely grated sharp Kraft Light Naturals cheese
15 oz. can	black or kidney beans, drained		
1/2 cup	water	2 oz.	Frigo Truly Light Mozzarella
1 pkg.	taco seasoning mix		
1/2 cup	cooked brown rice	3/4 cup	light sour cream
1 cup	frozen corn	3/4 cup	nonfat yogurt
		1 1/2 cup	salsa or hot sauce

Put turkey, chicken or beef, beans, water, taco seasoning mix, brown rice and corn in a saucepan. Simmer for 10 minutes. Wrap tortillas in foil, and warm in a 350 degree oven for 5 to 10 minutes, or wrap in a damp towel, and warm in the microwave, or warm on a hot griddle. Spoon filling into tortilla, top with a small amount of combined cheeses, some lettuce, tomatoes, salsa, and sour cream/yogurt mixture.

MENU SUGGESTION

W	12 oz.
V	CARROT AND JICAMA SALAD^
G	included tacos
F	tomatoes in taco
P	SOFT SHELL TACOS^

NOTES

MAIN DISHES

SPEEDY FETTUCINI WITH VEGETABLES
By Susan Stokes

Serves 4	Serving Size = 2 Cups	439 Calories	7 Fat Grams

1 cup	sliced carrots	1 can	Campbell's Healthy Request Low Fat Cream of Chicken (or Mushroom) Soup
1 cup	broccoli flowerets		
1 cup	cauliflower, small pieces		
1 medium	red bell pepper, chopped	1/2 cup	water
1 medium	onion, chopped	1 tsp.	dried basil, crushed
12 oz.	boneless, skinless chicken or turkey breast, cut into bite size chunks	8 oz.	fettuccine or other pasta cooked
		2 oz.	Kraft Light Naturals Swiss or Cheddar Cheese, shredded OR use slivered fat free singles (4 FG)

Spray a large non-stick fry pan with cooking spray. Stir-fry carrot over medium heat for 2 minutes. Add broccoli, cauliflower, pepper, and onion, and stir-fry 3 or 4 minutes longer. Remove vegetables from fry pan; add poultry and stir-fry 3 or 4 minutes or until opaque (add a teaspoon or so of water if meat starts to stick). Add soup, water, and basil to fry pan; mix thoroughly. Stir in vegetables. Bring to a boil; reduce heat, and add cheese. Cook and stir until cheese is almost melted.

Serve over hot pasta. Pass freshly grated Parmesan if desired.

MENU SUGGESTION

W	12 oz.
V	Tossed Mixed Greens with No or Low Fat Dressing
G	Whole Grain Bread or Roll
F	Fruit in Season
P	SPEEDY FETTUCCINE WITH VEGETABLES^

NOTES

SPICY "FRIED" CHICKEN
By Susan Stokes

Serves 4	Serving Size = 1 portion	153 Calories	3 Fat Grams

2 Tbl.	cornmeal	1/4 tsp.	ground Cumin
1 tsp.	paprika	4	skinned, boned chicken
1/2 tsp.	salt		breast halves
1/2 tsp.	onion powder		(about 1 lb. total)
1/4 tsp.	garlic powder	light coat	vegetable oil cooking spray
1/2 tsp.	pepper		

In a shallow dish, mix all of the dry ingredients. Rinse chicken, shake off excess water, but do not pat dry. Coat chicken evenly on all sides with the cornmeal mixture. Spray a cold skillet with cooking spray. Heat over medium-high heat. Cook chicken pieces for 8 to 10 minutes or until no longer pink, turning occasionally to brown evenly on all sides.

MENU SUGGESTION

W	12 oz.
V	OVEN FRIES^
G	Corn on the cob
F	Tomato slices
P	SPICY "FRIED" CHICKEN^

NOTES

MAIN DISHES

STACEE'S GONE ALL AFTERNOON STEW

By Susan Stokes

Serves 8   **Serving Size = 2 1/2 Cups**   **305 Calories**   **4 Fat Grams**

2 lbs.	lean top round steak trimmed of fat and cubed	1 can	Campbells Italian Tomato soup
1 Tbl.	dry tapioca	1/2 cup	water
5 medium	carrots, cut in chunks	1 tsp.	salt
4 oz.	fresh mushrooms, sliced	1/4 tsp.	pepper
3 large ribs	celery, thick sliced	1 bay leaf	
2 large	onions, cut in chunks	1/4 cup	red wine vinegar
4 medium	potatoes, cut in chunks	1 1/2 cup	frozen peas

Layer all ingredients except peas in a large heavy roaster. There is no need to brown meat first. Cover tightly (if lid is not heavy and snug - use aluminum foil).

Bake at 275 degrees for 5 hours. Stir in peas just before serving.

MENU SUGGESTION

W	12 oz.
V	SPINACH-CITRUS SALAD^
G	Whole Grain Bread or Roll
F	included in salad
P	GONE ALL AFTERNOON STEW^

STICKY CHICKEN

By Susan Stokes

Serves 8   **Serving Size = 1/2 Cup**   **280 Calories**   **3 Fat Grams**

2 lbs.	skinless, boneless chicken or turkey breast, all visible fat removed, cut into strips. (Cutting is easier if meat is partially frozen)
1 cup	apricot all fruit jam
1 cup	Fat Free Catalina Salad Dressing OR Barbecue Sauce
1 envelope	Lipton dry onion soup mix.

In a non-stick fry pan, over medium-high heat, saute the chicken strips until lightly browned . Combine the rest of the ingredients, stir to mix, and pour over the chicken. Bring to a boil, turn the heat low, partially cover (open vent in lid, or slightly angle lid on pan) simmer 15 to 20 minutes.

Serve chicken and some sauce over steamed rice. (brown or white)

MENU SUGGESTION

W	12 oz.
V	Broccoli/Cauliflower/Carrots
G	STEAMED BROWN RICE^, Whole Grain Bread or Rolls
F	BROILED PINEAPPLE ROUNDS^
P	STICKY CHICKEN^

TERRIFIC TURKEY "STIR-FRY"

By Susan Stokes

Serves 6   **Serving Size = 1 1/2 Cups**   **137 Calories**   **1 Fat Gram**

8 oz	skinless boneless turkey breast, cut into small pieces
1/4 cup	stir fry sauce
2 medium	onions, halved and slivered
1 large	green pepper, cut in strips
1 large	red pepper, cut in strips (optional)
3 ribs	celery, sliced
1 cup each	fresh broccoli/cauliflower/carrots or use frozen 20 oz. package
8 oz.	fresh mushroom pieces or canned
1 tsp.	chicken bouillon granules
2 Tbl.	cornstarch
1 cup	water
1 can	water chestnuts, drained and sliced

Cook turkey and onion in stir-fry sauce until turkey is opaque. Add all veggies, cover and steam for just a few minutes, until the veggies are just crisp tender and still brightly colored. Combine bouillon, cornstarch and water. Stir into meat and veggies, add water chestnuts until thick and bubbly. Serve over brown rice.

** **An** assortment of other vegetables taste wonderful in this. I love to add garlic, sliced zucchini, mung bean sprouts, shredded cabbage, and a little hot pepper sauce.

NOTE: Any of your favorite stir-fry recipes will be very easy to modify. Leave out the oil. Use a small amount lean poulttry or meat and lots of vegetables. Spray cold wok with vegetable oil spray, heat, stir fry vegetables then meat - if anything begins to stick, just add some broth. Continue as recipe directs.

MENU SUGGESTION

W	12 oz.
P	TERRIFIC TURKEY STIR FRY^
V	included in stir fry
G	STEAMED BROWN RICE^
F	Pineapple

NOTES

95

TIJUANA DELIGHT
By Gloria Woodward

Serves 6	Serving Size = 1/6 Portion	418 Calories	14.5 Fat Grams

1/2 lb.	ground beef (extra lean)	1 1/3 cup	water
1 medium	onion (chopped)	1 can (1lb.)	cream-style corn
1 cup	celery (chopped)	1 can (2 cups)	cooked kidney beans
1 clove	garlic (minced)	1 can(8 oz.)	tomato sauce
2/3 cup	cracked wheat (raw)	6	corn tortillas
2 Tbl.	Worcestershire sauce	1 cup	shredded cheese
4 tsp.	chili powder		

Brown ground beef, add onion, celery, garlic and cracked wheat and saute lightly. Add rest of ingredients except cheese and tortillas. Cook together 5 minutes. In a 2 quart round casserole dish, put 1 tortilla then 1 cup sauce and alternate layers until sauce and tortillas are all used. Top with cheese and bake uncovered 30 minutes at 350 degrees.

TOM TURKEY DIVINE
By Susan Stokes

Serves 8	Serving Size = 1 1/2 Cups	268 Calories	6 Fat Grams

1 1/2 lbs.	cooked turkey breast meat, cut into bite size chunks
1 1/2 lbs.	fresh broccoli spears (or asparagus) **
2 cans	Campbells' Healthy Request low fat Cream of Chicken Soup
2 tsp.	chicken bouillon granules
3 Tbl.	cornstarch
2/3 cup	fat free mayonnaise
1/3 cup	plain nonfat yogurt
2 Tbl.	fresh lemon juice
1/2 tsp.	curry powder
1/2 tsp.	dry mustard
1 oz.	Parmesan cheese, freshly grated (1/3 cup)
2 oz.	Kraft Light Naturals sharp cheddar cheese, grated
2 oz.	Frigo Truly Light Mozzarella cheese, grated
1 1/2 cup	crushed corn flakes

Steam vegetables until crisp tender (do not overcook). Spray a large shallow casserole with cooking spray, arrange well drained vegetable in dish, top with turkey. Stir soup, bouillon, cornstarch, and mayonnaise together. Cook in microwave or on top of stove just until mixture comes to a boil (stir often). Whisk lemon juice, curry powder, dry mustard, and Parmesan into yogurt. Combine soup and yogurt mixtures; pour sauce over turkey and sprinkle with cheddar and mozzarella cheese, top with corn flakes. Bake at 350 degrees for 30 to 35 minutes, or until hot and bubbly.

** **Can** use frozen (thawed and drained)

MENU SUGGESTION

W	12 oz.
V	TOM TURKEY DIVINE^
G	Brown Rice
V	Tossed Salad
F	Strawberries

TURKEY ENCHILADAS
By Susan Stokes

Serves 8	Serving Size = 1		168 Calories	3 Fat Grams

8 oz.	shredded poached turkey breast (chicken can also be used)		4 oz.	grated Frigo Truly Lite mozzarella, divide in half
4 oz. can	diced green chilies, drained		8	corn tortillas (softened in microwave)
1/2 cup	finely chopped green onion			
1 pkg.	Lawrey's Enchilada sauce		1/2 cup	light sour cream
8 oz.	tomato sauce			

Spray a shallow baking pan with Pam. Make sauce according to package directions. Spoon some sauce into the bottom and set aside. Stir shredded turkey, diced green chilies, half of the onion, and 1/3 cup sauce together. Spoon evenly onto corn tortillas, sprinkle with half of the cheese, roll up, place seam side down in prepared pan. Pour remaining sauce over the top, and sprinkle with remaining cheese. Bake at 350 degrees for about 20 minutes. Serve on shredded lettuce with a tablespoon light sour cream and a sprinkle of green onion.

TURKEY POT PIE
By Susan Stokes

Serves 6	Serving Size = 1 Pie		321 plus Calories	8 Fat Grams

2-1/2 cups	turkey broth, (reserve 1/2 cup)		1/4 tsp.	sage
1 large	onion, coarsely chopped		1	bay leaf
2 medium	potatoes, peeled and diced		1/2 tsp.	leaf thyme
2 large	carrots, peeled, sliced		6 Tbl.	Wondra flour
2 ribs	celery, sliced		2 cups	cooked turkey, cubed
1/2 - 3/4	teaspoon salt		1 tsp.	lemon juice
1/4 tsp.	pepper		1 cup	frozen peas

Biscuits:

1/2 cup	whole wheat flour		1 tsp.	sugar
1/2 cup	all purpose flour		1/4 tsp.	salt
2 tsp.	baking powder		3 Tbl.	margarine
1/4 tsp.	cream of tartar		1/3 cup	plain low-fat yogurt

Bring 2 cups broth to a boil in a large pan. Add prepared vegetables and seasonings. Bring back to a boil. Reduce heat, cover pan, and simmer 10 to 15 minutes, or until vegetables are barely tender. Whisk flour into reserved broth; add to vegetable mixture; cook on medium high heat until thick and bubbly. Remove bay leaf. Stir in turkey, taste, and adjust seasonings. Keep warm. Preheat oven to 450 degrees. Combine all of the dry ingredients in a bowl. Cut in margarine until crumbly. Add yogurt. Stir with a fork just until dough holds together. Knead gently 8 times. Pat out on a lightly floured surface to a 7 inch circle. Cut into 6 wedges. Stir lemon juice and peas into turkey-vegetable mixture; pour into a round 3 quart baking dish. Place biscuit wedges on top.

Bake for 12 to 15 minutes.

MENU SUGGESTION FOR UPPER AND LOWER RECIPES:

W	12 oz.	W	12 oz.
V	WARM CALICO SALAD^	V	SPINACH-CITRUS SALAD^
G	CORN TORTILLA CHIPS^	G	included in pie
F	Papaya Slices with Line	F	included in salad
P	TURKEY ENCHILADA^	P	TURKEY POT PIE^

MAIN DISHES

VEGETABLE-CHEESE CANNELLONI
By Susan Stokes

Serves 12   **Serving size = 3" x 3"**   **164 Calories**   **3 Fat Grams**

Please don't let the length of this recipe intimidate you. It is fairly quick, and very easy to put together. In fact, I can make the recipe much faster than I can type it!

16 Egg Roll Wrappers (24 wrappers per package)

TOMATO SAUCE:

1 medium	onion, finely chopped	1 pkg.	Schillings Thick and Zesty
1 clove	garlic, minced		Spaghetti Sauce mix
8 oz.	mushrooms, chopped fresh	1-3/4 cups	water
6 oz. can	tomato paste		

Spray a medium size non stick fry pan with cooking spray. Saute onion, garlic and mushrooms until they are softened, but not brown. Spoon half of the cooked vegetables into the large bowl you will use to make the filling. Stir tomato paste, spaghetti mix, and water into remaining vegetables; bring to a boil and simmer, stirring often, for 10 minutes. Remove from heat; set aside.

BECHAMEL SAUCE: (white sauce)

2 cups	skim milk	1/4 tsp.	salt
1/3 cup	instant nonfat dry milk	1 pkt.	Butter Buds (1/2 oz.)
3 Tbl.	Wondra flour		

Stir all ingredients together in a microwave safe 4 cup measuring cup. Microwave until thickened and bubbly. Stop microwave and stir sauce about every minute so that it will be nice and smooth. In my microwave this sauce takes about 5 minutes. Cover tightly with plastic wrap to keep skin from forming on top. Set aside. (This sauce can be made on the stove - stir constantly.)

FILLING: reserved cooked vegetables

2 cups	non-fat Cottage Cheese OR	1/4 tsp.	pepper
	non-fat Ricotta	1/2 tsp.	nutmeg
4 oz.	Frigo Truly Lite mozzarella	2	egg whites
	cheese, shredded	1 tsp.	salt
3 oz.	freshly grated Parmesan	10 oz. pkg.	frozen chopped
	(reserve 1/3 cup)		spinach, thawed and
3 Tbl.	fresh parsley, minced		squeezed almost dry
1/2 tsp.	dry leaf basil	1/3 cup	bechamel sauce

Add all of the filling ingredients to the reserved onion, garlic, and mushroom mixture. Stir until well combined.

METHOD:

Position top oven rack in the upper third of the oven. Preheat oven to 400 degrees. Spray a large shallow casserole dish or two 8x8 inch square baking pans with vegetable cooking spray. Spread 1 cup of the tomato sauce in the bottom of the prepared pan, or divide it between the 2 smaller pans. Lay an egg roll wrapper on a clean flat surface; put 1/4 cup of filling on top, and spread to cover the entire wrapper. Roll up, keeping it somewhat loose. Lay it in the prepared pan with its loose edge down. Proceed until all 16 wrappers are filled. Squeeze cannelloni in tightly if you have to, but don't overlap them. Spread the remaining tomato sauce over the filled cannelloni evenly. Drizzle the bechamel sauce over this. Sprinkle with the reserved 1/3 cup parmesan cheese. Bake for about 20 to 25 minutes, or until a very light golden crust forms on top. Remove from oven, and allow to stand 10 minutes before serving.

MENU SUGGESTION

W	12 oz.
V	MARINATED VEGETABLES^
G	Whole Grain Roll
F	Frozen Banana Slices
P	VEGETABLE-CHEESE CANNELLONI^

WHOLE WHEAT CHILI
By Gloria Woodward

Serves 6　　　**Serving Size = 1 1/2 Cups**　　　**285 Calories**　　　**4.3 Fat Grams**

1 lb.	95% lean ground beef	1/2 tsp.	salt
1 lg.	onion	1/2 tsp.	ground cumin
1 cup	celery (diced)	2 tsp.	chili powder
1 qt.	tomatoes (canned)	2 - 3 cups	cooked wheat berry kernels

Brown ground beef, onion and celery until beef is no longer red and vegetables are transparent. Drain well. Put in blender canned tomatoes (chopped-pulse blender twice). Add tomatoes, salt, cumin, chili powder, and cooked wheat berry kernels to meat and simmer until flavor is well blended. If too juicy, thicken with 2 tablespoons cornmeal or corn flour. If too thick, add a little more tomatoe juice or water.

VARIATION: Use ground beef, vegetables, tomatoes, 1 cup water and 1 package chili seasoning. Then add cooked wheat kernels.

YUMMY LAYERED CASSEROLE
By Susan Stokes

Serves 8　　　**Serving Size = 4 1/2" x 3 1/4"**　　　**304 Calories**　　　**4 Fat Grams**

12 oz.	Rotelle Macaroni	1 medium	green pepper, finely chopped
8 oz.	fat free cream cheese	26 oz. jar	Healthy Choice Spaghetti Sauce
1/4 cup	light sour cream		
1 cup	nonfat cottage cheese	8 oz.	*extra (95%) lean ground beef (cooked, drained, rinsed)
1 oz.	freshly grated parmesan		
1 medium	onion, finely chopped	2 oz.	Frigo Truly Light Mozzarella

MAIN DISHES

Stir spaghetti sauce and ground beef together, keep warm. Cook rotelle according to the package directions. Drain, rinse with cold water, and drain again. Spray a large flat 9" x 13" casserole dish with vegetable oil cooking spray. Put 1/2 of the cooked noodles in the dish. Combine cream cheese, sour cream, cottage cheese and parmesan cheese. Saute onion and pepper in a small non-stick skillet until barely tender, stir into cottage cheese mixture. Spread cheese mixture on top of noodles evenly. Put remaining noodles on top, cover with spaghetti sauce. Top with mozzarella and bake at 350 degrees for 30 minutes.

* **Ground** top round steak is a good alternative

MENU SUGGESTION

W	12 oz.
V	Green Beans
	Tossed Salad
G	Whole-grain Bread or Rolls
F	Frozen Banana Slices
P	YUMMMY LAYERED CASSEROLE^

FAVORITE PERSONAL RECIPES

MISCELLANEOUS

MISCELLANEOUS

BLENDED COTTAGE CHEESE - SOUR CREAM SUBSTITUTE
By Susan Stokes

Makes 1 Cup   **Serving Size = 2 Tbl.**   **18 Calories**   **0 Fat Grams**

This is my favorite substitute for sour cream in dips and dressings. I use yogurt and yogurt cheese a lot, but I do not car for them alone in veggie dips or dressings.

1 cup	nonfat cottage cheese
1 Tbl.	fresh lemon juice or buttermilk
1 Tbl.	nonfat yogurt

Blend in blender or food processor, scraping down several times, until absolutely smooth.

I like to make this at least several hours ahead and chill. It thickens, and the flavor mellows.

CANADIAN GUIDE FOR COOKING FISH
By Susan Stokes

METHOD

Measure fish at its thickest point. Allow 10 minutes cooking time per inch of thickness. Double the time if the fish is frozen. Lift a flake of fish and check the thickest part; fish is done when it is just opaque.

This works with any cooking method: broiling, poaching, grilling, etc.

CANDY

There are some very low fat candies that you can make at home, and some that you might want to buy occasionally. Here are two lists of possibilities. This is not a liscense to eat the whole bag.

CANDY TO BUY

Hard candy such as:	Chewy candy such as:	Candy to make:
Jolly Ranchers	Gumdrops	Marshmallow
Candy Canes	Jelly Beans	Divinity
Starlight Mints	Sour Balls	Taffy
Lifesavers	Swedish Fish	Suckers (Hard
	Licorice (some brands)	Candy)
	Marshmallow type candy	

MISCELLANEOUS

CRACKED WHEAT
By Gloria Woodward

Serving Size = 1 Cup W.W. Kernals   **570 Calories**   **3.3 Fat Grams**

METHOD IN A BLENDER

You can use your blender to crack wheat and other grains. Wheat kernals are hard and will take 25 - 35 seconds to crack. For fun make a mixture of several grains and crack them for a milti-grain flavor. Other grains are softer and only take 20-25 seconds. Try a mixture of grains available in your area.

In either case the method is the same. Place the blender on the blender drive and put 2/3 cup of grain kernels in it. Fit the lid snuggly in place and turn on to medium high speed for the desired number of seconds. Pour the cracked kernals into a fine sieve or onto a splatter screen placed over a large bowl. Work the kernals over the sieve to remove the flour particles. This is helpful in keeping your cooked cereal from becomming overly sticky. The cleaned cracked kernals are now ready to cook. The course flour portion can be added to your next batch of bread.

For cooking instructions, see the Breakfast Section in the CRACKED WHEAT CEREAL^.

DOUGH ENHANCER

If you have poor wheat you may wish to make your own dough enhancer. you may need to experiment with the amounts of the following ingredients to find the best results for the wheat you have

1 - 3 tsp.	Lecithin
2 - 4 tablets	Vitamin "C" 500 mg tablets (ground up prior)
1 Tbl. - 1/2 cup	w.w. gluten flour

Ingredients may be found in health food stores.

NOTES

EGG SUBSTITUTE
(Like Egg Beaters)
By Susan Stokes

Makes 6 Eggs   **Serving Size = 1 Egg**   **60 Calories**   **1.5 Fat Gram**

Dry Mix: 2-1/2 cups instant non-fat dry milk and 1 cup flour.

Whisk the following ingredients together:

1/3 cup	dry mix	1 tsp.	vegetable oil
1/4 cup	additional dry milk	as desired	yellow food coloring
6 large	egg whites		

This makes the equivalent of 6 large eggs. Refrigerate. Use within 3 days.

FISH IN A FLASH
By Susan Stokes

METHOD

Cooking fish is one of the things the microwave oven does best! It's easy, tasty, and moist—plus clean up is a snap. The following method adapts to almost any type of fish. Here is how to cook 1 pound of fillets to perfection:

Choose 1/2 inch thick fillets of white fish. Arrange fillets in a single layer in a 13 x 9 inch microwave dish. Sprinkle with Butter Buds and drizzle with 2 tablespoon fresh lemon juice. Cover loosely with wax paper. Microwave on high 2 minutes. Turn the dish halfway around; microwave 2 to 3 minutes more, until the fish is just opaque in the center. Let stand covered 2 minutes. Season with salt and pepper.

NOTES

MISCELLANEOUS

FOUR WAYS TO POACH CHICKEN
By Susan Stokes

METHOD

Skinless chicken breast = 3 FG per 4 oz. raw meat
Mixed dark and light poached chicken = 9 FG per cup of diced meat

#1. Poached Chicken

1	large fryer, cut up	1 tsp.	salt
1 qt.	cold water	1/8 tsp.	pepper
1 medium	onion, cut in 4 pieces	1/2 tsp.	basil leaves
1 rib	celery, 4 pieces	1 Tbl.	dry parsley
1	carrot, cut in 4 pieces		

Combine all of the ingredients in a deep pot. Cover and bring to a boil on high heat. Reduce heat, simmer until chicken is tender, about 1 1/2 hours. Remove from heat. Remove chicken pieces with a slotted spoon, cool. Strain broth and refrigerate so that fat hardens and can be easily removed. Remove chicken meat from bones, refrigerate and use within a day or two, or freeze for a quick meal later.

Note: One 3 to 4 pound fryer yields about 4 cups cooked cubed chicken. Consider buying 3 nice fryers when prices are good and triple the ingredients above. The broth and chicken freeze very well.

#2. Poached Chicken Breasts
Yields about 2 cups cooked cubed chicken.

1 1/2 cups	water
2 whole	chicken breasts (1 1/2 lbs.) skinned
1 1/2 t.	chicken bouillon

Put water in a large skillet; bring to a boil. Add chicken breasts; cover. Reduce heat and simmer 25 to 30 minutes, or until the chicken is tender and the juices run clear.

#3. Microwave Poached Chicken
2 whole chicken breasts, halved and skinned (1 1/2 lbs.)

Place chicken breast halves in a 2 quart microwave safe baking dish. Be sure thickest portions are toward the outside of the dish. Cover with wax paper. Microwave on high power 6 to 7 minutes. Turn meat over, cover and cook 6 or 7 more minutes, or until chicken is tender and the juices run clear.

#4. Oven Poached Chicken

Wrap individual chicken breast in aluminum foil packets. Place on a baking sheet. Bake at 350 degrees for 1 hour.

Idea: Sprinkle each piece of meat with a little chicken bouillon granules to obtain extra flavor.

MISCELLANEOUS

SEASONED BREAD CRUMBS
By Susan Stokes

127 Calories   **1.5 Fat Grams**

RECIPE #1

1/2 tsp.	marjoram leaves	1/8 tsp.	ground ginger
1/2 tsp.	garlic salt	1/4 cup	bread crumbs from
1/8 tsp.	black pepper		1 1/2 slices w.w. bread

RECIPE #2

1/4 cup	dry bread crumbs from 1 1/2 slices w.w. bread
1/4 tsp. each	pepper, sage, paprika and onion salt

SWEETENED CONDENSED MILK

Makes 3 Cups   **Serving Size = 1 Cup**   **621 Calories**   **2 Fat Grams**

1 cup	very hot tap water
4 cups	instant non-fat powdered milk
1 1/2 cups	fructose
1 Tbl.	Promise Ultra tub margarine
4 tsp.	Butter Buds

Put hot water and powdered milk into blender container, process briefly, turn off and scrape down sides of container. Process again, turn off and scrape sides again to make sure all of the powdered milk is dissolved. Turn the blender back on, and add the sugar through the opening in the lid while it is running. Turn off, scrape sides, blend again. Pour into a quart jar, or other container. Cover and refrigerate over night before using.

THOUGHTS ON PIE
By Susan Stokes

It is fairly simple to reduce the fat in many recipes and still have a nice texture in the finished product. Some recipes should not be "fooled with", and I personally feel that pie crust is one of them. What to do? Here are a few hints.

1. Have pie <u>occasionally</u> - watch your portion size - <u>enjoy it</u> when you do eat it!
2. Make 4 crusts (tops or bottoms) out of a standard 3 crust recipe (49 FG per crust instead of 65) use 1, freeze 3.
3. Make single crust pies - put fruit filling in unlined pie plate top with a crust.
4. Use low or lower fat fillings. Do not dot with butter" as many recipes direct. Use skim evaporated milk in place of regular evaporated milk (you save 19 grams of fat per cup).
5. Think creatively about reducing fat in favorite fillings, and eat tiny portions of the ones that can't be reduced (Pecan comes to mind).

YOGURT CHEESE
By Susan Stokes

Makes 3/4 - 2 Cups*　　　**Serving Size = 2 Tbl.**　　**27　Calories**　　　**0 Fat Gram**

Draining yogurt overnight makes a low-fat, high calcium alternative to cream cheese, or sour cream. It is very easy to do - once you discover some of the possibilities your only problem will be keeping it on hand. Substitute in most recipes calling for cream cheese, or use it in place of sour cream in stroganoff, dips, desserts, etc.

If you make yogurt cheese with vanilla yogurt, it will be slightly sweet - wonderful for fruit dips or dressing for fruit salad, or to use as a spread on bagels or toast.

Do not beat by hand, blender, mixer, or food processor. Let yogurt cheese come to room temperature before adding to hot mixtures.

* **16** oz. yogurt will make about 3/4 - 1 cup yogurt cheese
  32 oz. yogurt will make about 1 1/2 - 2 cups yogurt cheese.

* **Use** yogurt with no added gelatin.

DIRECTIONS:

8, 16 or 32 oz. container non-fat yogurt without added gelatin. Be sure to read the label!

3 tablespoons (blended until smooth) low fat cottage cheese per cup of yogurt (optional - for firmer, more stable yogurt cheese)

1 teaspoons fructose for every 2 cups yogurt (This does not sweeten it, just takes the sharpness away)

Line a colander with plain white light weight paper towel or a coffee filter, and set over a bowl. Stir yogurt, blended cottage cheese (if using), and Fructose together; spoon into lined colander. Cover with plastic wrap and refrigerate 12 to 18 hours until it reaches desired thickness. Spoon yogurt cheese into a storage bowl; cover and refrigerate. Discard whey that has drained into bowl.

Yogurt cheese will keep for about 1 week longer than the expiration date on the carton of yogurt used.

This is a good place to remind you about the fat content in some common dip ingredients.　　*Sour Cream: 1 Tbl. = 2.5 FG　　*Cream Cheese: 1 Tbl. = 5 FG
　　　　　　　　　*Mayonnaise: 1 Tbl. = 11 FG　　*Whipping Cream (fluid): 1 Tbl. = 6 FG

New nonfat products are constantly becoming available in these and many other food products.

NOTES

MISCELLANEOUS

107

FAVORITE PERSONAL RECIPES

SALADS

SALADS

BEET & ORANGE SALAD
By Susan Stokes

Serves 6   **Serving Size = 1 1/2 Cup**   **57 Calories**   **0 Fat Grams**

6 cups	fresh spinach
1 can	sliced beets (16 oz.)
2 medium	oranges cut in half and sliced
drizzle	SWEET AND SOUR DRESSING^

CARROT AND JICAMA SALAD
By Susan Stokes

Serves 8   **Serving Size = 1/2 Cup**   **42 Calories**   **0 Fat Grams**

Toss 2 cups each coarsely shredded carrots and jicama with 1/2 cup Fat-Free Catalina Salad Dressing.

CARROT - PINEAPPLE - RAISIN SALAD
By Susan Stokes

Serves 8   **Serving Size = 1/3 Cup**   **78 Calories**   **0 Fat Grams**

4 large	carrots, peeled and shredded
1/3 - 1/2 cup	plumped raising (pour boiling water over raisins, let stand 1 or 2 minutes, drain well)
8 oz. can	crushed pineapple in its own juice, well drained
1/2 cup	lemon yogurt
1/2 cup	Fat Free Miracle Whip

Toss carrots and raisin together. Stir crushed pineapple, yogurt and Miracle Whip together, pour over carrot mixture, toss to coat. Serve immediately. Shredded unpeeled apple also taste wonderful as an addition to this salad.

NOTES

SALADS

CHICKEN-COUSCOUS SALAD
By Susan Stokes

Serves 8	Serving Size = 1 1/4 Cup	220 Calories	2 Fat Grams

1-1/2 cup	couscous	1/2 cup	sliced green onion
1 lb.(3 cups)	shredded cooked chicken breast	3/4 cup	red bell pepper, chop
		6 Tbl.	minced fresh parsley
1 medium	cucumber, un-peeled, seeded, and coarsely chopped	1/2 cup	Wishbone Lite Italian salad dressing
1 medium	carrot, peeled and coarsely shredded	2 - 3 Tbl.	fresh lemon juice
		to taste	freshly ground pepper
1/2 cup	thinly sliced radish		

Put dry couscous and 1/2 teaspoon salt into a large serving bowl. Pour 2-1/2 cups boiling water over couscous. Cover bowl with a plate or piece of plastic wrap. Let stand 5 minutes. Uncover and cool for 15 minutes.

Add chicken and vegetables to couscous. Stir salad dressing and lemon juice together; pour over salad and toss to combine. Chill.

Serve on a pretty leaf of lettuce - grind fresh pepper on top.

MENU SUGGESTION

W	12 oz.
V	WARM AND SPICY TOMATO JUICE^
G	Ry-Krisp Crackers
F	Fruit Cup & SPICY RAISIN PUFFS^
P	CHICKEN-COUSCOUS SALAD^

CORN SALAD
By Gloria Woodward

Serves 8	Serving Size = 1/2 Cup	86 Calories	.6 Fat Grams

1 can	whole kernal corn, drained	1/2 cup	celery (chopped)
		1/2 cup	green peppers (chopped)
1 cup	tomatoes (diced)		
1 cup	cucumber (diced)	6	green onions (chopped)

Combine all of the above ingredients and then top with 3/4 cup Kraft "FREE" no-fat Italian or French dresing. Let chill for several hours stirring occasionally.

NOTES

SALADS

CREAMY COLESLAW
By Susan Stokes

Serves 6	Serving Size = 3/4 Cup	37 Calories	Fat Grams = t

4 cups	shredded cabbage	1 Tbl.	white wine vinegar
1 medium	carrot, grated	3 Tbl.	plain non-fat yogurt
3 Tbl.	fat free mayonnaise	1 Tbl.	apple juice concentrate (undiluted)

Put cabbage and carrots in a bowl. Whisk dressing ingredients together, pour over vegetables, and toss to coat.

CRISP RAINBOW SALAD
By Susan Stokes

Serves 6	Non-dressing Serving = 1 Cup	29 Calories	0.2 Fat Grams

1-1/2 cups	finely shredded red cabbage	1-1/4 cups	finely shredded green cabbage
1-1/2 cups	shredded jicama**		
1-1/2 cups	shredded carrot	1/3 cup	minced fresh parsley

Use No or Low Fat Salad Dressing (try Bernstein's LIGHT FANTASTIC Creamy Dijon) Toss green cabbage and parsley together. Arrange shredded vegetables, side by side on a serving platter. First red cabbage, then jicama, carrots, and finally cabbage/parsley mix. Serve by scooping from each side toward the center with two large spoons.

** **Jicama** (pronounced hic-a-ma) is a tuberous root with a rough thick brown skin and white, crisp, slightly sweet flesh. It can be eaten raw in salads or with dip, or can be used in a stir fry to replace water chestnuts. It can usually be found with the more "exotic" items in the produce department. Jicama should feel heavy for its size; avoid those with soft moldy spots.

FRUITED COLESLAW
By Susan Stokes

Serves 6	Serving Size = 1 1/2	132 Calories	Fat Grams = t

6 cups	shredded cabbage	1/4 cup	Fat Free Miracle Whip
2 sliced	banana	1/3 cup	plain non-fat yogurt
15 oz. can	pineapple tidbits	1 Tbl.	Lemon Juice
diced	apple or raisins if desired	2 Tbl.	Pineapple juice concentrate (undiluted)

Whisk Salad dressing, yogurt, lemon juice, and pineapple concentrate together. Pour over cabbage and fruit, and toss gently to coat.

SALADS

JICAMA-CARROT SLAW IN PEPPER RINGS
By Susan Stokes

Serves 10	Serving Size = 1/3 Cup	48 Calories	Fat Grams = t

2 cups	peeled shredded jicama	2 Tbl.	fat free mayonnaise
1 1/4 cup	shredded carrot	1/2 - 3/4 tsp.	salt
3 Tbl.	sliced green onion	3/4 tsp.	chili powder
2 Tbl.	lime or lemon juice	1/8 tsp.	pepper
1/4 cup	plain non-fat yogurt	2 large	green or red peppers cut
1/4 cup	light sour cream		into 10 thick rings

Pat shredded vegetables between paper towels to remove excess liquid. transfer to a bowl and toss in onion and lime juice. Mix remaining ingredients in a small bowl; stir into vegetables, cover and chill

To serve, spoon into center of pepper rings.

PASTA PRIMAVERA SALAD
By Susan Stokes

Serves 8	Serving Size = 1 Cup	166 Calories	2 Fat Grams

10 oz. pkg.	Rainbow Rotini (macaroni)
8 oz. bottle	Wishbone Lite Italian Salad Dressing
1/4 cup	sliced green onions
2 Tbl.	freshly grated parmesan cheese
1 cup each	broccoli flowerettes, carrot slices, cauliflower

The following ingredients are optional, you can vary them to suit your family's taste.

Artichoke hearts (in water not oil)   Sliced Mushrooms
Water chestnuts   Cauliflower Pieces*
Chopped Red or Green Pepper   Chopped Celery
Sliced Zucchini Garbanzo, Kidney or black beans
(Tuna, Shrimp, Crab of Chicken will turn this into a Main Dish.)

Cook the Rotini according to pkg. Instructions. Drain and rinse with cold water, drain well and put into a large bowl; add salad dressing, green onions, vegetables and parmesan cheese. Toss to mix. Add any or all of the optional ingredients, toss and serve.

* NOTE: Broccoli, carrots, or cauliflower can be steamed for 3 or 4 minutes, then plunged into ice water, (or use a bag of thawed frozen); drain well before adding.

MENU SUGGESTION

W	12 oz.
V	PASTA PRIMAVERA SALAD^
G	Whole-grain Rolls
F	Sliced Melon
P	Broiled Chicken

SALADS

QUICK AND EASY FRUIT SALAD
By Susan Stokes

Serves 8	**Serving Size = 3/4 Cup**	**149 Calories**	**0 Fat Grams**

15 1/4 oz. can	pineapple tidbits in their own juice—do not drain
3 1/2 oz. pkg.	instant lemon pudding mix or vanilla or banana cream pudding mix
1 can	lite fruit cocktail, drained
1 can	mandarin oranges, drained
1 medium	sliced banana
1 cup	red or green seedless grapes
1 medium	diced unpeeled apple

Stir pudding mix into pineapple and juice in a large bowl. Fold in all of the fruit. Serve Immediately.

MENU SUGGESTION

W	12 oz.
V	Sliced Tomatoes
G	Whole grain Bread or Rolls
F	QUICK AND EASY FRUIT SALAD^
P	FISH DINNER IN FOIL^

REFRIGERATOR COLESLAW
By Susan Stokes

Serves 24	**Serving Size = 1/2 Cup**	**47 Calories**	**0 Fat Grams**

1 medium	head cabbage, shredded	1 cup	vinegar
1 medium	onion, chopped	3/4 cups	honey
1 medium	red pepper, chopped	1 tsp.	mustard seed
1 medium	green pepper, chopped	1 tsp.	celery seed
1 large	carrot, shredded		

Put vegetables in a large bowl, cover with cold water, stir in 1 Tablespoon salt. Let stand in refrigerator for 1 hour. Drain well, add chilled dressing, mix well, store in the refrigerator. This will keep for weeks!

Dressing: Combine vinegar, honey, mustard see, and celery seed in a stainless steel saucepan. Bring to a boil, then chill before pouring on vegetables.

NOTES

SALADS

SPINACH-CITRUS SALAD
By Susan Stokes

Serves 8   **Serving Size = 1 1/2 Cup**   **38 Calories**   **Fat Grams = t**

5 cups	torn spinach	1 can	grapefruit sections,
4 cups	torn leaf lettuce		drain (or fresh grapefruit)
1 can	mandarin orange sections, drained (or fresh orange)	1 small	red onion, thinly sliced & separated into rings

In a large salad bowl combine spinach, lettuce, orange sections, grapefruit sections, and onion. Add SWEET AND SOUR DRESSING^ . Toss to coat; serve immediately.

TURKEY SALAD WITH A TWIST
By Susan Stokes

Serves 44   **Serving Size = 1 1/2 Cup**   **294 Calories**   **3 Fat Grams**

SALAD		DRESSING	
3 cups	turkey breasts, chopped, cooked	1/3 cup	nonfat mayonnaise
1 large	red apple, skinned, diced	1/3 cup	plain nonfat yogurt
1 large rib	celery, diced	1 1/2 Tbl.	honey
3/4 cup	cranberries, coarsely chopped	4 tsp.	spicy brown mustard
		1/2 tsp.	dried Marjoram leaves
		1/8 tsp.	white pepper
		1/8 tsp.	ground ginger
		1 tsp.	lemon juice

Combine salad ingredients in a large bowl. Combine dressing ingredients in a small bowl.   Whisk until blended. Pour dressing over salad and stir gently.

MENU SUGGESTION

W	12 oz.
V	Baked Yam
G	Whole Grain Roll
F	Included in Salad
P	TURKEY SALAD WITH A TWIST^

TURKEY - RICE & APPLE SALAD
By Susan Stokes

Serves 8   **Serving Size = 1 1/3 Cup**   **180 Calories**   **2 Fat Grams**

This is a great way to use some left-over Thanksgiving turkey. Use the recipe for WALDORF SALAD in this book. Omit walnuts and Grapenuts, and add the following ingredients:

2 cups	cooked turkey, breast meat, cubed	1/4 cup	green onion, sliced
2 cups	cooked brown rice	to taste	salt & pepper

Double dressing ingredients, pour over salad; stir gently to mix well. Cover and chill until serving time. Serve on a mixture of lettuce, spinach and sprouts. Garnish with green onion if desired.

MENU SUGGESTION

W	12 oz.
V	CREAM OF PUMPKIN SOUP^
G	Whole Grain Roll
F	included in salad
P	TURKEY - RICE & APPLE SALAD^

SALADS

WALDORF SALAD
By Susan Stokes

Serves 8   **Serving Size = 3/4 Cup**   **97 Calories**   **2 Fat Grams**

2 medium	red apples, diced	1 large rib	celery, sliced
2 medium	green apples, diced	2 Tbl.	chopped walnuts
1 cup	seedless red grapes, cut in half	2 Tbl.	Grapenuts cereal
		to taste	CREAMY DRESSING^

Combine apples, grapes, celery, and walnuts in a serving bowl. Pour on Creamy Dressing; stir gently to mix well. Cover and refrigerate until serving time. Just before serving, stir in Grapenuts.

CREAMY DRESSING

1/2 cup	non-fat lemon yogurt	1/2 tsp.	finely grated lemon peel
1/4 cup	Kraft Fat Free Mayonnaise	1 Tbl.	honey

Stir all ingredients together until smooth.

WARM CALICO SALAD
By Susan Stokes

Serves 8   **Serving Size = 3\4 Cup**   **112 Calories**   **1 Fat Gram**

1 tsp.	olive oil	10 oz. pkg.	frozen corn, thawed
1 1/2 cups	chopped onion	1/2 tsp.	salt
1 clove	minced garlic	1/8 tsp.	pepper
3/4 cup	chopped green pepper	2 Tbl.	non-fat Italian Salad Dressing
3/4 cup	chopped red bell pepper	2 tsp.	lime juice
16 oz. can	black beans, rinsed and drained	8 small	red cabbage leaves

Heat oil in a large non-stick fry pan. Add onion, garlic, green and red pepper; saute' 4 or 5 minutes. Add all remaining ingredients except cabbage "cups". Cook and stir for 2 or 3 minutes, or until heated through. Serve in cabbage cups.

NOTES

SALADS

SIDE DISHES

SIDE DISHES

BAKED POTATO CREAMY TOPPING
By Susan Stokes

Serves 4 - 6　　　**Serving Size = 3 Tbl.**　　　**30 Calories**　　　**0 Fat Grams**

1/3 cup	Fat Free Peppercorn Ranch Salad Dressing (Kraft)
3/4 cup	plain non-fat yogurt
1 or 2 Tbl.	finely chopped green onion or chives

Blend all ingredients well, serve over baked potatoes.

BAKED YAMS AND APPLES
By Susan Stokes

Serves 10　　　**Serving Size = 1/2 Cup**　　　**84 Calories**　　　**Fat Gram = t**

1 cup	pineapple or apple juice	1/4 tsp.	cinnamon
1-1/2 Tbl.	cornstarch	3 medium	apples, sliced
1/8 - 1/4 tsp.	salt	2 cups	(1 - lb.) sliced, cooked
1/4 cup	honey		or canned yams
1 tsp.	lemon juice		

Combine juice, cornstarch, salt and honey in a small saucepan. Cook over medium heat stirring frequently until mixture is thick and bubbly. Add lemon juice and cinnamon. Spray a 1 quart casserole dish with cooking spray. Alternate layers of apples and yams in the dish. Pour the hot sauce over, and sprinkle lightly with a little more cinnamon. Bake at 400 degrees for 1 hour or until apples are tender. (Baking in the microwave shortens the time on this cover loosely with wax paper and microwave 15 to 20 minutes. Rotate 1/4 turn every 5 minutes or use turntable.)

BROWN RICE PILAF
By Susan Stokes

Serves 6　　　**Serving Size = 1/2 Cup**　　　**49 Calories**　　　**.5 Fat Grams**

1/2 tsp.	salt		
1/4 tsp.	dried basil	1/2 cup	finely chopped celery
1/4 tsp.	dried thyme	1/2 cup	finely chopped onion
1/4 tsp.	dry mustard	1/2 cup	finely chopped carrot
1/4 tsp.	freshly ground pepper	1 clove	minced garlic
1/4 tsp.	paprika	1 cup	long grain brown rice
1/8 tsp.	cayenne pepper	2 cups	water

Combine first seven ingredients in a small bowl. Spray a large saucepan with Pam; add chopped vegetables and cook until crisp tender. Stir in brown rice and saute for 2 or 3 minutes (stir often.) Add reserved seasoning mixture and 2 cups water. Bring to a boil, reduce heat to low and cook for 5 minutes. Cover, and steam for 40 minutes without lifting lid.

BULGUR PILAF
By Susan Stokes

Makes 8	Serving Size = 1/2 cup	129 Calories	1 Fat Grams

2-1/4 cups	low-sodium chicken broth	1/2 tsp.	dry thyme leaves, crush
1 large	onion, finely chopped	1-1/2 cups	bulgur wheat
1 rib	celery, finely chopped	1-1/2 tsp.	soy sauce
1 med.	carrot, finely chopped		

Combine all ingredients in a large fry pan. Bring to a boil. Reduce heat, cover and simmer 15 to 20 minutes, stirring once, until liquid is absorbed and bulgur is tender.

CABBAGE WEDGES WITH CHEESE SAUCE
By Susan Stokes

Serves 6	Serving Size = 1 Wedge with 3 Tbl. Sauce	96 Calories	1 Fat Gram

1-1/4 lb.	head of cabbage	1/8 tsp.	pepper
2 Tbl.	water	1 cup	skim evaporated milk
1/8 tsp.	salt	1/2 pkt.	Butter Buds
1 Tbl.	cornstarch	3 Tbl.	freshly grated Parmesan
1/4 tsp.	paprika	6 slices	Borden Fat Free Swiss
pinch	garlic powder		Singles, slivered
1/8 tsp.	salt	1/2 tsp.	dried dillweed

Remove the outer leaves from the cabbage. Cut cabbage into 6 wedges. Place cabbage in a single layer in a shallow microwave dish. Sprinkle with water and salt. Cover with plastic wrap, turn back one corner a little bit for a vent. Micro on high for 10 to 12 minutes, or until cabbage is tender, turn dish a quarter turn after 6 minutes. Drain cabbage well, set aside and keep warm. In a 2 cup glass measure combine cornstarch, seasonings, and milk. Cook uncovered, on high for 3 or 4 minutes or until thick and bubbly. Stir after every minute. Stir in cheeses, stir until melted. Serve sauce over cabbage wedges. Sprinkle with dillweed.

NOTES

CHEESY POTATOES
By Susan Stokes

Serves 12	Serving Size = 3" x 3"	125 Calories	3 Fat Grams

2 lb. bag	frozen, hash brown potatoes**, thawed or cooked and diced potatoes	2 tsp.	dry parsley
		1/2 cup	light sour cream
		1/2 cup	low-fat plain yogurt
1 can	Campbell's Healthy Request, Reduced Fat, Cream of Mushroom Soup	1 medium	onion, finely chopped or 1 cup chopped green onions
1 pkt.	Butter Buds	3 oz.	Kraft Light Natural Sharp Cheese***
1/2 tsp.	dry mustard		
1/2 tsp.	salt	1 oz.	Parmesan cheese
1/4 tsp.	pepper	2 cups	crushed corn flakes (use as a topping)
8 oz.	fat free cream cheese		

Spray a 9 by 13 inch baking dish with nonfat cooking spray. Mix all of the ingredients, except the corn flakes. Put potato mixture into prepared baking dish. Top with crushed corn flakes. Bake at 350 degrees for 45-50 minutes.

** **Be** sure to read package label, some hash browns are coated with fat. Cooked, shredded or cubed potatoes can be substituted.

*** **Try** using 3 or 4 oz. of fat free processed cheese slices (cut into slivers) to replace Kraft Light Naturals. YUMMY!! Kraft, Bordon, and Alpine Lace all sell this kind of cheese product. Using this substitution, each serving would contain 2 grams of fat.

COUSCOUS WITH VEGETABLES
By Susan Stokes

Serves 6	Serving Size = 1 Cup	182 Calories	Fat Grams = t

Couscous is made from ground durum wheat (seminola flour) and water, rubbed into small pellets, and pre-cooked. Look for couscous in small boxes on the health food aisle, import aisle, by the rice, or sometimes in the bulk food section. Couscous is an ancient food - probably one of the original FAST FOODS!

1 1/2 cups	carrot, shredded coarse	1 1/2 cup	couscous
2 cups	zucchini, shredded coarse	1/4 cup	finely minced fresh parsley
1/2 cup	onion, finely chopped	1 - 2 Tbl.	fresh lemon juice or to taste
1/2 cup	celery, finely chopped	1/2 tsp.	freshly grated black pepper
2 cups	chicken broth		

Spray a large non-stick fry pan with cooking spray. Stir fry carrot, celery, squash, and onion for 8 to 10 minutes (until liquid released from the vegetables evaporates). Add broth, bring to a boil, then stir in couscous. Remove from heat, cover and let stand for 5 minutes. Stir in parsley, lemon juice, and pepper. Serve immediately.

Note: Plain couscous can be prepared by adding 1-1/3 cup boiling liquid, (water, broth, milk), 1/4 to 1/2 teaspoon salt, and 2 teaspoons Butter Buds to 1 cup couscous. Stir. Cover and allow to stand for 5 minutes. Fluff with a fork. Couscous can be served as a grain side dish, like rice, or serve under Stir Fry, Ratatouille, Spaghetti Sauce etc. or add green onion, bell pepper, celery, minced parsley, rinsed and drained canned black beans and non-fat Italian salad dressing for a quick Pasta Salad.

SIDE DISHES

CRAN-APPLE YAM BAKE
By Susan Stokes

Makes 16	Serving Size = 1/2 Cup	139 Calories	Fat Grams = t

4 cups	(2 lbs.) sliced, cooked or canned yams	3 Tbl.	apricot jam (all fruit)
		3 Tbl.	orange marmalade (low sugar)
21 oz. can	apple pie filling		
16 oz. can	whole-berry cranberry sauce	1 tsp.	lemon juice

Spray a shallow 2 quart casserole with cooking spray. Spread pie filling in bottom of dish; arrange sliced yams on top. In a small mixing bowl, stir remaining ingredients together; spoon over yams. Bake, uncovered in a 350 degree oven about 25 minutes or until heated all the way through. (Or use microwave and less time.)

CRUNCHY FOUR GRAIN MIX
By Susan Stokes

Serves 16	Serving Size = 1/2 cup	75 Calories	.4 Fat Gram

This is a terrific grain dish - nutty tasting!

5 cups	water	3/4 cup	brown rice
1-1/4 tsp.	salt	1/2 cup	quick cooking barley
1/2 cup	bulgur wheat	1/4 cup	millet

Combine all ingredients in a heavy four quart saucepan. Bring to a boil, reduce heat to medium, boil for 5 minutes. Reduce heat to a very low setting, cover and steam for 40 minutes.

Freeze left-overs in serving size containers for a quick start on another meal.

EGG ROLLS

Finely chop a combination of vegetables (cabbage, bean sprouts, onion, celery, mushrooms, carrots, spinach) and chicken or shrimp. Spray a wok with cooking spray, stir fry vegetable/meat mixture. Moisten with broth and a touch of soy sauce, thicken with cornstarch. Taste and adjust seasoning. Cool. For each Egg Roll, lay 2 stacked sheets of Fillo on a clean flat surface, spray lightly with cooking spray. Fold in half crosswise, and lightly spray again. Put 1/4 of a cup of the cooled vegetable and meat mixture close to the edge (leave an inch or so) nearest you. Fold both sides toward the center, then carefully roll up to enclose the filling. Place on a baking sheet. Work quickly to fill the baking sheet. Spray egg rolls lightly with cooking spray. Bake at 350 degrees 15 to 20 minutes, or until golden brown.

NOTES

SIDE DISHES

FRUIT & VEGETABLE CASSEROLE
By Jean Shepherd

Serves 4	Serving Size = 3/4 Cup	86 Calories	0 Fat Grams

4 small	carrots, cut into thin sticks	1/2 cup	apple juice
2 medium	tart apples, thick sliced	dash	salt
	(Jonathan or Granny Smith)	dash	nutmeg
2 slices	red onion (thick)	dash	cinnamon

Place the carrots in an 8x8 inch baking dish. Arrange apple slices on top of carrots. Separate onion slices into rings and arrange over apples slices. Pour apple juice into baking dish. Sprinkle with salt, nutmeg and cinnamon. Cover tightly with foil. Bake at 350 degrees for 45 minutes.

JICAMA WITH LIME JUICE
By Susan Stokes

Serving Size = 1/2 Cup	25 Calories	Fat Grams = t

1 medium	jicama, peeled and rinsed	3	limes, juiced (about 1/4 cut)
to taste	shredded lettuce	1/2 tsp.	chili powder

Cut jicama into 1/4 inch slices, then cut the slices into 2 x 1/4 inch sticks. Place on shredded lettuce. Sprinkle with lime juice, then sprinkle on chili powder. Cover and chill until served.

LOW-FAT MACARONI AND CHEESE
By Susan Stokes

Serves 4	Serving Size = 3/4 Cup	180 Calories	1 Fat Gram

It is easy to lower the fat in boxed macaroni and cheese! Just use skim milk (or skim evaporated milk), and increase amount by 2 or 3 tablespoons - leave out all butter or margarine. Add 1/2 package Butter Buds if desired. (1/2 package equals 4 level teaspoons.) Be aware that some macaroni and cheese boxes contain MSG. Smith's brand contains no MSG.

NOTES

MARINATED VEGETABLES
By Susan Stokes

Serves 8   **Serving Size = 3/4 Cup**   **43 Calories**   **1 Fat Grams**

2 large	carrots, peeled and sliced diagonally into 1/4 inch slices
2 cups	fresh cauliflower flowerets
9 oz. pkg.	frozen Italian-style green beans
1/2 cup	No or Low-Fat Italian salad dressing
1 large	red bell pepper cut into chunks
1 small	Red onion sliced and seperated into rings

Steam carrots and cauliflower briefly, until crisp-tender. Cook beans according to pkg. directions, omitting the salt. Drain vegetables. Place in a large bowl. Add salad dressing, red pepper chunks, and onion slices. Toss until vegetables are coated. Cover and chill for 4 hours or longer.

OVEN FRIES
By Susan Stokes

Serving Size = 1 potato   **220 Calories**   **0 Fat Grams**

Heat oven to 425 degrees. Spray a large baking sheet with Vegetable Oil Cooking Spray. Scrub, but do not peel, baking potatoes (at least one per person) Cut each potato in half lengthwise, then into 1/2 inch wide wedges. Rinse in cold water; spread potatoes on pan in a single layer. Spray potato wedges with Pam and sprinkle with desired seasoning. Bake 25 to 30 minutes, until lightly browned and tender. A whole potato has only a trace of fat.

SUGGESTED SEASONINGS:

Salt
Seasoned salt, plain or spicey
Garlic or Onion Salt
Taco Seasoning mix
Cajun Seasoning

NOTES

SIDE DISHES

PINEAPPLE GREEN BEANS
By Susan Stokes

Serves 4   **Serving Size = 2/3 Cup**   **46 Calories**   **0 Fat Grams**

1 lb.	green beans (fresh or frozen) cooked until crisp tender in small amount of water	1/2 cup	finely chopped onion
		4 tsp.	cornstarch
		1 1/2 Tbl.	soy sauce
1 cup	pineapple juice		

Drain beans, reserving cooking liquid. Add pineapple juice to reserved liquid, to make 1 1/2 cup. Pour into sauce pan, add onion, cornstarch, and soy sauce. Cook, stirring constantly until thickened. Add beans; heat through.

SKINNY MASHED POTATOES
By Susan Stokes

Serves 6   **Serving Size = 1/2 Cup**   **47 Calories**   **0 Fat Grams**

2 lbs.	potatoes (6 medium)	as needed	skim evaporated milk
1 pkt.	Butter Buds		

Cook potatoes in lightly salted water until tender. Drain, add 1 packet Butter Buds, and skim evaporated milk as needed. Whip until smooth.

STEAMED BROWN RICE
By Susan Stokes

Serves 8   **Serving Size = 1/2 cup**   **110 Calories**   **Fat Grams = t**

2 cups	water	1/2 tsp.	salt
1 cup	brown rice		

Rinse rice and drain. Put into saucepan with water and salt. Bring to a boil turn heat low, simmer uncovered for 5 minutes, stir, cover: and cook on low heat for 40 minutes - don't peak! Fluff with a fork before serving.

I usually make a triple batch of rice - it heats up very nicely in the microwave, and I can always find a lot of ways to use it.

NOTE: Soaking brown rice overnight cuts the cooking time down to about 25 or 30 minutes.

NOTES

SIDE DISHES

STUFFED BAKED POTATOES
By Susan Stokes

Serves 8   **Serving Size = 1**   **132 Calories**   **1 Fat Grams**

You can store stuffed potatoes in the freezer for up to three months.

4 large	baking potatoes	1/3 cup	parmesan cheese
1 small	onion, finely chopped	1/8 tsp.	nutmeg
1 cup	non-fat cottage cheese	1/4 tsp.	pepper
1/4 cup	skim evaporated milk combined	to taste	paprika
	with 1/2 tsp. lemon juice	1/4 cup	finely sliced chives or
1 pkt.	Butter Buds		green onion
4 oz.	fat free cream cheese	to taste	salt

Heat oven to 400 degrees. Scrub potatoes, and pierce in several places with a fork. Place on oven rack and bake about 1 hour, or until tender.
Cook onion in a large non-stick fry pan until tender but not brown. Add a little water if onion starts to stick. Cut baked potatoes in half lengthwise. Carefully scoop out pulp (be very careful not to tear skin), mash - don't worry about small lumps - add to onions in fry pan. Stir in cottage cheese, milk, Butter Buds, cream cheese, parmesan cheese, nutmeg, and pepper. Stir over medium heat until warm, taste and adjust seasonings. Stuff back into shells; sprinkle with paprika. **Bake** at 375 degrees 15 minutes. Sprinkle with green onions just before serving or Stuff, cool, cover with foil, freeze. Bake in a 400 degree oven for 20 minutes, remove foil and bake another 10 minutes.

TEX-MEX RICE
By Susan Stokes

Serves 8   **Serving Size = 3/4 Cup**   **185 Calories**   **Fat Grams = t**

1 1/2 cup	long grain brown rice	add	water
1 large	onion, chopped	2 tsp.	chicken bouillon granules
2 cloves	garlic, minced	1 1/2 tsp.	chili powder
16 oz. can	tomatoes and juice	1/2 tsp.	ground cumin

Spray the sauce pan with Pam nonstick cooking spray. Saute' onion and garlic until slightly softened. Drain tomatoes, reserving liquid. Add the water to re-served tomato liquid until you have 3 1/2 cups liquid total. Coarsely chop tomatoes and add to onions. Stir in remaining ingredients. Bring to boil. Turn heat to low and steam for 50 - 55 minutes. No peeking!

NOTES

SIDE DISHES

FAVORITE PERSONAL RECIPES

SNACKS - APPETIZERS

BAGEL CRISPS
By Susan Stokes

Cut bagels as thin as possible (easier if partieally frozen). Follow same method as for Pita Crisps.

CORN TORTILLA CHIPS
By Susan Stokes

Serves 6   **Serving Size = 16 Wedges**   **76 Calories**   **1 Fat Gram**

For the lightest possible crunch, buy a package of corn tortillas that contains 12 tortillas, and weighs 8 ounces.

Cut tortilla into 8 wedges; lay in a single layer on a baking sheet. Sprinkle lightly with desired seasoning. Bake at 350 degrees for about 10 minutes. these can also be done in th microwave.

SUGGESTED SEASONINGS:

Salt, Seasoned Salt, Taco Seasoning Mix, Mollly McButter Cheese flavored sprinkles

EMILY'S LOW FAT NACHOS
By Susan Stokes

Serves 4   **Serving Size = 16 Chips**   **196 Calories**   **3 Fat Grams**

64	homemade tortilla chips	4 Tbl.	plain non fat yogurt
2 oz.	Frigo Truly Lite mozzarella cheese, shred (about 1/2 cup lightly packed)	4 Tbl.	lite sour cream
4 slices	Kraft Free Singles, slivered	1	green onion finely chopped
to taste	Salsa	Chopped	pickled jalapenos

INSTRUCTIONS:

Stir lite sour cream, yogurt, and green onions together; set aside. Crowd the corn chips on a cookie sheet or oven proof platter. Scatter the cheeses over the chips and put in the oven or micro. until the cheese melts. Scatter the chopped jalapeno over the nachos according to taste. **Serve** immediately with salsa and sour cream mixture.

SERVING SUGGESTIONS:
* Serve these as a hearty snack, OR, make them a meal by adding nonfat refried beans and seeded diced tomato to the nachos.
* Serve with a large Mixed Greens and Veggie Salad.
* For dessert, try a DESSERT SHELL: fill with drained peaches and non-fat frozen vanilla yogurt, drizzle with caramel topping.

NOTES

FLOUR TORTILLA CHIPS
By Susan Stokes

Both Villa Victoria and Lynn Wilson make flour tortillas with 1 gram of fat each. **Read the label!** If it does not say how much fat is in each tortilla, you can figure 5 grams each.

Cut the flour tortillas into wedges; lay on bakeing sheet. Spray very lightly with Pam, or mist with water. Sprinkle with desired seasoning. Bake at 350 degrees for about 10 minutes or lay wedges on a paper towel; microwave for about 1 1/2 minutes, rotate 1/4 turn, microwave 1 minute longer.

SUGGESTED SEASONINGS:
Salt
Seasoned Salt
Taco Seasoning Mix
Cinnamon and Fructose

FRENCH BREAD CRISPS
By Susan Stokes

Slice bread thin. Lay on racks and leave out overnight. (This works great here in the dry West - in a more humid area, dry in a very low oven, or on paper towels in the microwave.)

FRESH FRUIT WITH LEMONY DIPPING SAUCE
By Susan Stokes

Serves 8   **Serving Size = 1 Cup Fruit**   **82 Calories**   **0 Fat Grams**

Assorted Fresh Fruit:
Banana Slices
Pineapple Chunks
(fresh or canned)
Seedless grapes
Strawberries
Peach slices

Apple Slices
Orange Sections
(fresh or canned
Kiwi slices
Melon
Pear wedges

Dipping Sauce:
8 oz.   Non-fat Lemon Yogurt
1/4 - 1/2 tsp.   finely grated lemon or line peel (optional)

NOTES

HELEN'S LITE CANDIED POPCORN
By Susan Stokes

Serves 32   **Serving Size = 1 cup**   **111 Calories**   **1 Fat Grams**

This treat is addictive! Be sure to measure out your treat and put the rest away!

8 quarts	air popped corn
2 cups	C&H brown sugar, firmly packed
1 cup	light corn syrup
2 Tbl.	butter or margarine
1 tsp.	salt
1 tsp.	vanilla
1/2 tsp.	baking soda

Spray a large metal bowl or pan with cooking spray; pour in popped corn, put into a 250 degree oven to keep warm while you make the syrup. Combine brown sugar, corn syrup, butter, Butter Buds and salt in a heavy saucepan. Bring to a boil stirring constantly. Boil 5 minutes. Stir vanilla and soda together in a small bowl. When syrup has cooked 5 min., remove pan from heat, and stir in vanilla mixture (syrup will go foamy). Pour hot syrup over warm popcorn; stir gently to coat. Bake for 1 hour at 250 degrees. Stir every 15 minutes. Remove from oven and immediately pour out onto counter - break apart and let cool. Store in an air-tight container.

MOTHER GOOSE POPCORN
By Susan Stokes

Serves 32   **Serving Size = 1 cup**   **126 Calories**   **1 Fat Grams**

One of my childhood favorites. My Granny used to fix it every Christmas.

8 quarts	air popped corn	1/2 tsp.	cream of tartar
4 cups	granulated sugar	2 Tbl.	butter or margarine
1 cup	water	1/4 tsp.	food coloring flavoring extract - optional

Combine sugar, water, cream of tartar, margarine, and food coloring; stir. Bring to a boil. Boil 4 minutes; remove from heat, stir in flavoring if desired, and let stand 4 or 5 minutes. Pour over popcorn and stir until popcorn goes sugary.

Note: Try using 1 teaspoon of an extract, or a drop or two of oil (such as cinnamon). It is fun to have a certain color of popcorn have a particular flavor.

NOTES

ORIENTAL APPETIZER
By Susan Stokes

Serves 10 **Serving Size = 1/4 Cup** **16 Calories** **Fat Grams = t**

1 cup	finely chopped, cooked chicken or turkey breast	1/3 cup	chopped jicama, or water chestnuts
1/4 cup	sliced green onions	1 Tbl.	chopped fresh parsley
1/4 cup	diced red bell pepper	1/4 tsp.	ginger
2 tsp.	soy sauce	1/2 - 3/4 cup	sweet and sour sauce
1/2 - 1 tsp.	Mrs. Dash Garlic & Herb seasoning		(bottled or use the book recipe)
1/2 cup	shredded carrot	8 oz.	fat free cream cheese

In a medium bowl combine all ingredients except sweet and sour sauce, cream cheese and sour cream; mix well. Cover and refrigerate several hours to blend the flavors.

Stir cream cheese and sour cream together and spread over the bottom of a 10 inch serving dish. Spoon chicken/vegetable mixture evenly over yogurt cheese. Drizzle with sweet and sour sauce.

Serve with low or no fat crackers - homemade or purchased.

PITA CRISPS
By Susan Stokes

Makes 16 Wedges **1 Whole Pita = 1 Fat Gram**

Cut whole wheat pita bread into wedges. Separate each wedge in two; lay on baking sheet. Sprinkle lightly with salt or any desired seasoning. Bake at 350 degrees for about 10 minutes.

POTATO CHIPS
By Susan Stokes

Scrub, but do not peel a baking potato. Slice in uniform thin slices. Rinse with cold water, shake off excess. Spray a microwave bacon rack with Pam. Lay potato slices on rack in a single layer. Sprinkle lightly with desired seasoning. Microwave on high power for 8 to 10 minutes. Rotate 1/4th turn after 5 minutes. They will be crisp and pale brown with a few darker spots.

There is only a trace of fat in a whole potato.

SUGGESTED SEASONINGS:

Salt
Seasoned salt
Garlic salt
Onion salt
Taco seasoning mix
Cheese flavored sprinkles
Sour cream and chive flavored sprinkles
Cajun seasoning mix blended with a little salt.

SAVORY SPINACH PINWHEELS
By Susan Stokes

Serves 20   **Serving Size =3 Appetizers**   **75 Calories**   **1.5 Fat Grams**

4 oz.	Kraft Light Naturals sharp cheese (1 cup, lightly packed)	1/2 tsp.	garlic powder
2 - 3 Tbl.	finely chopped green onion	8 oz.	fat free cream cheese
5 oz. can	water chestnuts, drained and finely chopped	1/2 cup	light sour cream (1 g. fat per Tbl.)
10 oz. pkg.	frozen chopped spinach, thawed and very well drained (squeeze moisture out)	1/4 cup	finely chopped red bell pepper
		6 - 10 inch	flour tortillas (FG = 1 ea.)

Wrap tortillas in plastic wrap and warm in the microwave just to soften (or use foil and put in the oven). In a medium bowl, stir together all ingredients except tortillas. Lay a tortilla on a clean flat surface, spread with about 1/2 cup spinach mixture. Roll up tightly; wrap in plastic wrap. Refrigerate at least 2 hours or until set.

To serve: Remove plastic wrap; cut each rolled appetizer into 10 slices.

SEAFOOD PARTY APPETIZER
By Susan Stokes

Serves 10   **Serving Size = 4 Vegetables**   **127 Calories**   **Fat Grams = t**
                                            4 Crackers
                                            1/4 Cup Dip

8 oz.	fat free cream cheese	3 Tbl.	sliced green onions
12 oz.	imitation crab or lobster or shrimp	4 Tbl.	chopped green pepper
2/3 cup	seafood cocktail sauce	4 kinds	crackers (*see list below)
		4 kinds	vegetables (*see list below)

Stir cream cheese and sour cream together. Spread in the center of a large tray (1/2" - 3/4" thick). Shred crab into a strainer, rinse with cold water, drain; pat between paper towels to remove excess water. Top cream cheese mixture with crab then drizzle with seafood sauce and sprinkle on onions and peppers. Pile vegetables and crackers around edges of the tray.

Variation: Use shrimp or a combinaton of crab and shrimp. Use salsa instead of seafood sauce, serve with tortilla chips.

* **Celery** sticks, thick red and green bell pepper strips, jicama slices, cucumber rounds.

* **Homemade** Pita Crisps or Tortilla Chips or Mr. Phipps Pretzel Chips RyKrisp or Wheat Krisp or Melba Toast or Nabisco Snack Well Wheat Crackers.

SEASONING IDEAS FOR "CRACKERS" AND "CHIPS"
By Susan Stokes

Taco seasoning mix (pour dry mix into a shaker)
Spicy season all (seasoned salt)
Hidden Malley Ranch dressing mix (pour dry mix into a shaker)
Cajun seasoning
Molly McButter Cheese Flavor Sprinkles (plain or on top of taco seasoning)
Molly McButter Sour Cream and Chives flavor sprinkles

WONTON CHIPS
By Susan Stokes

5 Wonton Wrappers = 1 Fat Gram

Wonton wrappers can be found in a refrigerated case near the produce department in most grocery stores.

Cut wonton wrappers in half. Line baking sheet with foil and spray with Pam. Lay wonton wrappers on prepared pan. Mist lightly with water. Sprinkle with desired seasoning. Bake at 340 degrees for 9 to 11 minutes. *Be careful not to over brown.*

Suggested seasonings are the same as the Flour Tortilla's: salt, seasoned salt, taco seasoning mix, cinnamon and fructose

ZIPPY SHRIMP COCKTAIL
By Susan Stokes

Serves 15	Serving Size = 2/3 Cup		49 Calories	Fat Grams = t
8 cups	tomato juice	1 cup	catsup	
*4 1/4 oz.	can shrimp, rinsed and drained	1/8 tsp.	garlic powder	
1 Tbl.	fructose	1/8 tsp.	onion powder	
1 Tbl.	horse radish	1/2 cup	diced celery	
1/4 cup	sliced green onion	1 Tbl.	worcestershire sauce	

Combine all ingredients in a non-metallic container. Cover and chill at least 12 hours. Serve in punch cups.

* Or use imitation crab.

NOTES

133

FAVORITE PERSONAL RECIPES

SOUPS - SAUCES

SOUPS & SAUCES

CHEESY WHITE SAUCE
By Susan Stokes

Serves 4	Serving Size = 1/3 Cup	88 Calories	2 Fat Grams
1 small	onion, finely chopped	4 tsp.	Butter Buds
1 small	clove garlic, minced	1 tsp.	chicken bouillon granules
2 Tbl.	Wondra	1 tsp.	dried basil
3/4 cup	skim evaporated milk	4 Tbl.	parmesan cheese, freshly grated

Spray a small saucepan with vegetable oil cooking spray. Saute onion, and garlic over medium heat, stirring constantly, until the onion is translucent. Whisk flour and milk together, pour into pan with onion. Add bouillon and Molly McButter, cook, stirring constantly until thickened. Stir in Parmesan Cheese. Serve over pasta or rice.

NOTE: This is seasoned. If you want plain white sauce, leave out the onion, garlic, basil and parmesan.

CLAM CHOWDER
By Susan Stokes

Serves 6	Serving Size = 2 Cup	135 Calories	2 Fat Grams
2 cans	minced clams (6 oz.)	1/3 cup	cornstarch
2 medium	potatoes	3/4 cup	skim milk
1 medium	onion, finely chopped	1 large can	skim evaporated milk
2 ribs	celery, finely chopped	1 t.	salt
1	carrot, chopped	1/4 - 1/2 tsp.	pepper
2 tsp.	fish bouillon	1/2 t	fructose
1 packet	Butter Buds (1/2 oz.)	1 Tbl.	lemon juice
1/3 cup	non-fat dry milk		

Drain liquid from both cans of clams into a 4 or 5 quart saucepan. Add bouillon, all of the vegetables, and enough water to barely cover them. Bring to a boil, turn head down and simmer, covered, for about 15 minutes or until vegetables are tender. Sprinkle dry milk and Butter Buds over the vegetables, stir gently to dissolve. Stir together skim milk and cornstarch, add this along with the can of skim evaporated milk to the cooked vegetables. Bring back to a boil, stirring constantly. Add salt, pepper, sugar, lemon juice and reserved clams. Stir together, simmer 5 minutes to blend flavors.

MENU SUGGESTION

W	12 oz.
V	Coleslaw
G	Whole Grain Bread or Rolls
F	Sliced Green Apples
P	CLAM CHOWDER^

COOKS CHOICE SYRUP
By Gloria Woodward

Serves 12   **Serving Size = 3 Tbl.**   **42 Calories**   **0 Fat Grams**

Measure about 1 1/2 cup water in blender. Then add frozen juice concentrate, fresh fruit or other juice to a total measurement of 2 cups. Add 1/2 cup sugar and 2 tablespoon instant clear jel (instant modifiied food starch) with blender running.

If you do not have access to clear jel, substitute it with 2 1/2 to 3 tablespoons cornstarch and cook ingredients over medium heat until thickened.

CRANBERRY ORANGE SAUCE
By Susan Stokes

Makes 3 Cups   **Serving Size = 2 Tbl.**   **35 Calories**   **0 Fat Grams**

This is my very favorite cranberry sauce! Wonderful with turkey, chicken, or extra lean ham. Be sure to chill well (preferably over night) so it sets up.

1 cup	orange juice
1 1/2 cup	fructose or sugar
12 oz. pkg.	fresh cranberries, sorted and rinsed

Bring juice and fructose or sugar to boil in a 4 quart saucepan (this foams up). Add cranberries; reduce heat, put lid on pan, and cook until all of the cranberries pop. Remove lid, stir, simmer 5 minutes. Cool.

CREAM OF PUMPKIN SOUP
By Susan Stokes

Serves 6   **Serving Size = 1 1/2 Cups**   **145 Calories**   **1 Fat Grams**

1 medium	onion, chopped	1/8 tsp.	pepper
1 medium	celery rib, chopped	1 small	bay leaf
1 medium	carrot, peeled and chopped	1/4 tsp.	leaf marjoram, crushed
1 medium	potato, peel and dice	1/4 tsp.	leaf thyme, crushed
16 oz. can	pumpkin, OR 1-1/2 cups cooked	3 Tbl.	Wondra flour
	mashed pumpkin or	1 cup	skim evaporated milk
	winter squash	1/4 cup	light sour cream
3 cups	chicken broth (reserve 1/2 cup)	to taste	salt (optional)

Spray a large saucepan or Dutch oven with cooking spray. Cook onion and celery until tender, stirring often (if they start to stick, add a little water.) Add carrot, potato, pumpkin, 2-1/2 cups broth, and all seasonings. Bring to a boil, turn down and simmer for 30 minutes. If a smooth soup is desired, puree in blender or food processor in batches. Return pureed mixture to pan. Stir flour into reserved broth; add to soup, bring back to a boil, stirring constantly. Turn heat to low. Stir in skim evaporated milk and light sour cream, heat through, but do not boil.

MENU SUGGESTION

W	12 oz.
V	Salad
G	Whole Grain Roll or Bread
F	CRANBERRY-PEAR COBBLER^
P	CREAM OF PUMPKIN SOUP^

CUSTARD SAUCE
By Susan Stokes

Serves 10	Serving Size = 1/4 Cup	58 Calories	0 Fat Grams

1 pkg.	instant (4 serving size) vanilla pudding	2-1/2 cups 1/4 tsp.	skim milk rum extract

Beat all ingredients together. Serve separately to pour over each serving.

DESSERT IDEAS USING CRANBERRY SAUCE
By Susan Stokes

1. Serve over a scoop of lemon or orange sherbet.
2. Serve over a scoop of non-fat vanilla yogurt or vanilla ice milk.
3. Serve over a slice of angel food cake.
4. Serve on top of tapioca pudding.
5. Layer with vanilla pudding for a parfait.

FRESH FRUIT WITH LEMONY DIPPING SAUCE
By Susan Stokes

Serves 8	Serving Size = 1 Cup Fruit	82 Calories	0 Fat Grams

Assorted Fresh Fruit:

Banana Slices	Apple Slices
Pineapple Chunks	Orange Sections
(fresh or canned)	(fresh or canned
Seedless grapes	Kiwi slices
Strawberries	Melon
Peach slices	Pear wedges

Dipping Sauce:
8 oz.   Nonfat Lemon Yogurt
1/4 - 1/2 tsp. lemon or line peel finely grated (optional)

FRUIT COCKTAIL SAUCE
By Susan Stokes

Serves 12	Serving Size = 1/4 Cup	31 Calories	0 Fat Grams

16 oz. can	fruit cocktail, drained, reserve juice	1/2 cup 1/3 cup	fructose cornstarch
1 1/4 cups	water	pinch	salt
2 Tbl.	fresh lemon juice		

Stir dry ingredients together in a small saucepan; add liquids and stir until smooth. Cook over medium heat stirring constantly until thickened and clear; stir in fruit cocktail. Serve warm over gingerbread.

FRUIT SAUCES
By Susan Stokes

Try drizzling one of these sauces over the season's best fruits.

SAUCE #1

Serves 8	Serving Size = 2 Tbl. each	48 Calories	Fat Grams = t

4 oz.	fat free tub cream cheese	1/2 tsp.	vanilla
1 1/2 Tbl.	honey	1/4 cup	light sour cream
1/4 cup	plain non-fat yogurt		

Beat cream cheese, brown sugar, and vanilla until fluffy. Add yogurt; beat until smooth. Drizzle over fruit..

SAUCE #2

Serves 8	Serving Size = 2 Tbl. each	46 Calories	.5 Fat Grams

4 oz.	fat free tub cream cheese	1/4 cup	plain nonfat yogurt
1/4 cup	light sour cream	1 or 2 Tbl.	orange all fruit jam
	(1 gram fat per tablespoon)	to taste	marmalade

Stir together. Especially nice served over combination of pineapple chunks, banana, orange sections and grapes.

SAUCE #3

Serves 8	Serving Size = 2 Tbl.	18 Calories	0 Fat Grams

8 oz.	Nonfat VANILLA or
8 oz.	Nonfat LEMON Yogurt

SAUCE #4

Makes 8	Serving Size = 3 Tbl. each	36 Calories	0 Fat Grams

1 cup	nonfat cottage cheese	1 Tbl.	lemon juice
1/2 cup	orange juice	2 Tbl.	honey
1/4 tsp.	finely grated orange peel - optional		

In a blender at high speed, blend the cottage cheese, orange juice, lemon juice, brown sugar, and orange peel until smooth.

LEMON SAUCE
By Susan Stokes

Makes 8 Servings	Serving Size = 2 Tbl.	29 Calories	1 Fat Gram

1/3 cup	fructose	1 1/2 tsp.	butter
4 tsp.	Butter Buds	1/2 tsp.	grated lemon peel
1 Tbl.	cornstarch	1 1/2 Tbl.	fresh lemon juice
1 cup	water	pinch of	salt

Combine sugar and cornstarch in a small saucepan; stir well. Add remaining ingredients. Cook over medium heat, stirring constantly, until mixture is thick and glossy.

LENTIL VEGETABLE SOUP
By Susan Stokes

Serves 8	Serving Size = 2 Cups	118 Calories	2.5 Fat Grams

2 cups	dry lentils	1/4 tsp.	pepper
4 medium	carrots, sliced	6 cups	HAM BROTH^
2 large ribs	celery, sliced	8 oz.	extra lean cooked ham,
1 large	onion, chopped		diced (1-1/2 cups)
1/4 tsp.	marjoram leaves	4 cups	canned tomatoes, cut up
2 medium	potatoes, diced		

Combine lentils, carrots, onion, celery, seasonings, and broth in a large pan. Bring to a boil. Reduce heat; cover and simmer 1 hour. Stir in ham and tomatoes; simmer 15 minutes.

HOW TO DE-FAT HAM AND BEAN SOUP

Any recipe you have that calls for Ham Hock or Ham Shank (or other meat or poultry bones) can be modified by using the following instructions:

1. Cover a large meaty ham shank with about 3 quarts cold water. Add 1 teaspoon of salt and a large bay leaf and bring to a boil. Reduce heat and simmer for 2-1/2 to 3 hours; skim foam off top of broth several times during the first hour of cooking. The trick is to simmer not boil! (Boiling a meat broth causes the fat to be absorbed into the broth; making the broth cloudy and fatty.)

2. Leave the ham shank submerged in the broth; cool and then refrigerate overnight.

3. Sort and rinse desired beans; cover with room temperature water and leave on the counter overnight.

4. Remove solid fat from the top of the broth. Warm broth enough to remove ham shank. Cut lean meat from bone (discard anything that is fatty). Dice the lean ham and return it to the broth.

5. Drain soaking water from beans, and use the de-fatted ham broth as the liquid your recipe calls for to cook the beans in - add water only if needed to cover the beans.

There is only a trace of **fat per cup** of broth and ham.

This method, using other herbs and seasonings, onion, celery, carrot etc. can be used to make nearly fat free broth from turkey bones, beef bones, chicken pieces etc.

MENU SUGGESTION

W	12 oz.
V	LENTIL VEGETABLE SOUP^
	Crunchy Red and Green Bell Pepper Strips
G	Whole Wheat Bread
F	BROILED PINEAPPLE ROUNDS^
P	Included in Soup

MINESTRONE SOUP
By Susan Stokes

Serves 6		Serving Size = 2 Cup		258 Calories		3 Fat Grams

1 large	onion, sliced		1 tsp.	oregano
2 cloves	garlic, minced		1 tsp.	salt
2 ribs large	celery, sliced		1/4 tsp.	pepper
2 large	carrots, sliced		2 cans	kidney beans (15 oz.)
1 can	Italian plum tomatoes (28 oz.)		2 cups	shredded cabbage
4 cups	defatted chicken broth		1 medium	zucchini, sliced
1 Tbl.	dry parsley flakes		1/2 cup	uncooked macaroni
2 tsp.	leaf basil		6 Tbl.	grated parmesan cheese

Spray a large sauce pan with Pam, heat over medium heat. Add onion, garlic, carrots, and celery. Saute, stirring often until onion is tender. Add tomatoes (break up any large chunks). Stir in broth and seasonings. Bring to a boil, reduce heat, cover and simmer 20 minutes. Add cabbage and drained kidney beans, simmer 10 minutes. Stir in zucchini and macaroni, simmer uncovered 10 minutes. Serve with 1 tablespoon freshly grated parmesan cheese on top.

MENU SUGGESTION

W	12 oz.
V	Relish Plate
	LOW-FAT VEGGIE DIP^
G	Whole grain Bread or Rolls
F	BAKED APPLES^
P	MINESTRONE SOUP^

PANCAKE PEAR SAUCE
By Gloria Woodward

Serves 16	Serving Size = 1/4 Cup	36 Calories	0 Fat Grams

In blender puree 1 quart bottles pears and while doing so add 1 1/2 to 2 tablespoon instant clear jel (instant modified food starch). Variations can be made from peaches, fruit cocktail, apricots, etc.

If clear jel is not available, substitute 2 1/2 to 3 tablespoons of cornstarch and heat over a medium temperature until thickened to your desire.

NOTES

PORTUGUESE BEAN SOUP
By Vicki Robison

Serves 6		Serving Size = 1 cup		147 Calories		Fat Grams = t
1 cup	dried red beans			1/4 tsp.	allspice	
6 cups	water			1 can	tomato paste(6 oz. can)	
1	onion (diced)			1/2 tsp.	salt	
1	clove (minced)			3 tsp.	beef bouillon	
3	potatoes (scrubbed & diced)					

Soak beans overnight. Drain beans then put them in crockpot with 6 cups water and cook on high about 2 hours. Add remaining ingredients and cook on low until tender. (About 2 to 3 hours)

I have also put everything together at the same time and cooked on high for 3 to 4 hours when I was not going to be home to add them seperately.

Generally beans should be cooked until they are tender before adding any acid based ingredients such as tomatoes or vinegar. The acids seem to interfere with the tenderizing of the beans.

QUICK AND EASY SAUCE
(use for Pasta or Pizza)
By Susan Stokes

Serves 6		Serving Size = 1/3 Cup		29 Calories		Fat Grams = t
28 oz. can	tomatoes, drained			1/4 tsp.	salt	
1/4 cup	tomato paste			1/8 tsp.	pepper	
1 tsp.	fructose			1/4 tsp.	garlic powder	
1 Tbl.	dried basil leaves			1 - 1 1/2 tsp.	onion powder	
1 Tbl.	parsley flakes					

Combine all ingredients in blender or food processor. Blend until smooth. Heat and serve on pasta, or use as a pizza sauce. Store in refrigerator for 1 week.

NOTES

SWEET AND SOUR SAUCE
By Susan Stokes

Serves 10   **Serving Size = 2 1/2 Tbl.**   **22 Calories**   **0 Fat Grams**

3 T	fructose	2 tsp.	cornstarch
1 cup	pineapple juice	1/4 cup	catsup
2 Tbl.	vinegar	2 tsp.	soy sauce
2 - 3 drops	hot pepper sauce		

Combine ingredients. Cook until thick, stirring frequently. Cool.

TERRIFIC PASTA SAUCE
By Susan Stokes

Serves 12   **Serving Size = 1/2 Cup**   **51 Calories**   **1 Fat Gram**

Marinara Sauce

1 1/2 tsp.	olive oil	6 oz. can	tomato paste
1 large	onion, coarsely chopped	1 tsp.	fructose
8 oz.	fresh mushrooms, sliced	3	cloves garlic, minced
2 Tbl.	dried basil leaves	1	bay leaf
	(6 Tbl. If using fresh basil)	to taste	salt
28 oz. can	tomatoes crushed	to taste	pepper
8 oz. can	tomato sauce		

Heat a large saucepan (at least 5 quart) over medium heat. Put oil, onion, mushrooms, basil, and garlic into pan. Cook, stirring often until onions are translucent. Add all the remaining ingredients except salt and pepper. Bring sauce to a boil, reduce heat, and simmer the sauce for about 1 hour, stirring occasionally. Add the salt and pepper, simmer 10 more minutes. Serve over hot pasta.

NOTES

VEGETABLE & TWO BEAN CHILI
By Susan Stokes

Serves 6   **Serving Size = 2 Cups**   **314 Calories**   **1 Fat Gram**

The method of browning and intensifying the flavors of the vegetables in this recipe is called BRAISE AND DE-GLAZE. It is a wonderful way to add rich flavor to soups, casseroles, etc. without adding fat.

1 large	onion, chopped	1/3 cup	bulgur wheat*
1 large	carrot, grated	1 can	tomatoes (35 oz.)
1 small	zucchini, grated	8 oz can	tomato sauce
1 medium	potato, grated	1 Tbl.	chili powder, to taste
1 large bud	garlic, minced	1/2 - 1 tsp.	ground cumin
1 cup	beef broth or bouillon	1/2 tsp.	pepper
2 cans	kidney beans (16 oz.)	if needed	salt
2 cans	black beans(16 oz.)	to taste	bay leaf

Spray a large saucepan with cooking spray. Put onion, carrot, zucchini, potato, garlic and 3/4 cup broth into a large, 5 quart saucepan. Turn heat to high and boil the liquid away rapidly. Stir, especially when liquid is almost gone. When vegetables begin to caramelize on bottom of pan (be careful, don't let them burn), add 1 tablespoon broth, stir a few seconds until it evaporates; add another tablespoon broth - repeat two more times. Remove pan from heat, add drained and rinsed beans, bulgur, tomatoes, tomato sauce and seasonings. Bring to a boil, breaking up tomatoes with a wooden spoon. Reduce heat, simmer uncovered 20 to 30 minutes.

Taste and adjust seasonings.

* **Bulgur** wheat can sometimes be found in the bulk section or import aisle in the supermarket, or at Health Food Stores.

OPTIONAL - This chili can be topped with 1 tablespoon light sour cream, 1 tablespoon sharp Kraft Light Naturals cheese, and chopped green onion.

These toppings add: 60 calories, 2 FG, 103 mg. sodium, and 9 mg. cholesterol per serving.

Try serving Chili over baked potatoes, polenta (corn meal mush), rice, couscous, or pasta.

MENU SUGGESTION

W	12 oz.
V	(Included in Chili), No or Low Fat Salad Dressing
G	Whole Grain Rolls or Bread
F	SPINACH-CITRUS SALAD^, Mixed Fruit Cup
P	VEGETABLE & TWO BEAN CHILI^

NOTES

MENU PLANS

Menus serve a family of four. **W** = Water, **V** = Veggie, **G** = Grain, **F** = Fruit, **P** = Protein

DAY 1

•	FG	BREAKFAST
W		12 oz.
V		see snack
G	3	3 WHOLE WHEAT PANCAKES^
F	t	all fruit jam,
		1/2 cup fresh raspberries
P	t	1/4 cup
		nonfat vanilla yogurt

SNACK

W		12 oz.
V	t	cut-up veggies

LUNCH

W		12 oz.
V	t	carrot strips
G	2	2 slices w.w. bread
F	t	banana
P	3	3 oz. tuna sandwich with
		nonfat mayonnaise

SNACK

W		12 oz.
G	t	2 popcorn rice cakes
V	t	cauliflower

DINNER

W		12 oz.
V	1	MARINATED VEGETABLES^
G	1	whole grain roll
F	t	frozen banana slices*
P	6	2 VEGETABLE-CHEESE
		CANNELLONI^

SNACK

W		12 oz.
G	2	1 cup Wheat Chex Cereal
P	t	8 oz. skim milk
V	t	carrot sticks

* slice, individually freeze, package and
use within three weeks.

DAY 2

•	FG	BREAKFAST
W		12 oz.
V	t	8 oz. V-8 juice
G	4	2 APPLESAUCE
		BRAN MUFFINS^
F	t	banana
P	t	1 cup nonfat
		vanilla yogurt

SNACK

W		12 oz.
V	t	sliced green pepper

LUNCH

W		12 oz.
V	t	tomato, wheat
		sprouts, leaf lettuce
G	t	2 slices rye bread
F	t	kiwi, strawberries
P	5	5 oz. chicken
		breast, mayon-
		naise, mustard,
		vegies sandwich

SNACK

W		12 oz.
V	t	1 cup steamed corn
		& peas with Butter
		Buds

DINNER

W		12 oz.
V	t	tossed salad,nonfat
		dressing, steamed
		cauliflower/petite
		peas
G	2	2 w.w. rolls
F	1	EASY BAKED APPLES^
P	4	ANGELA'S SHEPHERD
		PIE^

SNACK

W		12 oz.
G	4	2 APPLESAUCE-BRAN
		MUFFINS^
V	t	celery sticks

TOTAL FAT GRAMS: 18	TOTAL FAT GRAMS: 20

DAY 3

•	FG	BREAKFAST
W		12 oz.
V		see snack
G	2	1 c Oat Bran cereal
F	t	1/2 grapefruit
P	t	8 oz. skim milk

SNACK

•	FG	
W		12 oz.
G	t	2 popcorn rice cakes
V	t	vegies cut-up

LUNCH

•	FG	
W		12 oz.
V	t	tomato, lettuce
G	2	2 w.w. bread
F	t	apple
P	6	2 oz. turkey breast

SNACK

•	FG	
W		12 oz.
G	2	1 APPLESAUCE-BRAN MUFFIN^

DINNER

•	FG	
W		12 oz.
V	2	GREEN TOMATO RATATOUILLE^
G	1	1 whole grain rolls
	1	1/2 cup STEAMED BROWN RICE^
F	0	melon & PINEAPPLE BANANA SORBET^
P	3	2 Tbl. parmesan cheese

SNACK

•	FG	
W		12 oz.
F	t	grapes
P	t	1 cup nonfat lemon yogurt
V	t	cut-up veggies

TOTAL FAT GRAMS: 19

DAY 4

•	FG	BREAKFAST
W		12 oz.
V		see snack
G	2	1 cup Cheerios
F	t	banana
P	t	1 cup skim milk

SNACK

•	FG	
W		12 oz.
V	t	6 oz. V-8 Juice
	t	celery sticks

LUNCH

•	FG	
W		12 oz.
V	t	OVEN FRIES^
G	2	2 w.w. toast
F	t	tomato slices
P	4	8 oz. low-fat cottage cheese

SNACK

•	FG	
W		12 oz.
G	2	1 APPLESAUCE-BRAN MUFFIN^
V	t	carrot sticks
P	t	1/2 cup nonfat frozen vanilla yogurt

DINNER

•	FG	
W		12 oz.
V	t	sliced tomatoes
G	1	1 w.w. bread
F	t	QUICK & EASY FRUIT SALAD^
P	4	4 oz. Atlantic Halibut FISH DINNER IN FOIL^

SNACK

•	FG	
W		12 oz.
G	2	1 cup Wheat Chex
F	t	1 cup mixed fruit cup
P	t	6 oz. skim milk

TOTAL FAT GRAMS: 17

DAY 5

DAY 6

•	FG	BREAKFAST
W		12 oz.
V		see snack
G	3	1 1/2 cup oatmeal
F	t	peach slices
P	t	6 oz. skim milk

SNACK

W		12 oz.
V	t	broccoli/cauliflower

LUNCH

W		12 oz.
V	t	baked potato with
		Butter Buds
G	4	2 FRUIT FILLED BRAN
		MUFFINS^
F	t	1/2 c strawberries
P	2	1/2 c low-fat cottage
		cheese

SNACK

W		12 oz.
G	1	1 w.w. roll with all
		fruit jam
V	t	cucumber pieces

DINNER

W		12 oz.
V	3	CHEESY POTATOES^
	t	1 cup steamed
		broccoli
G	2	2 w.w. rolls
F	2	WALDORF SALAD^
P	3	CRUNCHY BAKED
		CHICKEN^

SNACK

W		12 oz.
G	2	1 cup cheerios
P	t	6 oz. skim milk

TOTAL FAT GRAMS: 22

•	FG	BREAKFAST
W		12 oz.
V	t	8 oz. V-8 Juice
G	4	3 W.W. PANCAKES^
		all fruit jam
F		included in topping
P	t	6 oz. skim milk

SNACK

W		12 oz.
V	t	cherry tomatoes, celery

LUNCH

W		12 oz.
V	4	10 3/4 oz. vegetable
		beef soup
G	2	2 w.w. rolls
F	t	banana
P		included in soup

SNACK

W		12 oz.
F	2.5	EMILY'S LOW FAT
		NACHOS^
V	t	vegies cut-up

DINNER

W		12 oz.
V	t	salad, nonfat drsg.
G	2	2 w.w. rolls
F	t	SPINACH-CITRUS
		SALAD^
P	2	2 servings QUICK
		VEGETABLE & TWO
		BEAN CHILI^

SNACK

W		12 oz.
G	2	1 cup Wheat Chex
		cereal
P	t	6 oz. skim milk

TOTAL FAT GRAMS: 18.5

DAY 7

.	FG	BREAKFAST
W		12 oz.
V		see snack
G	8	2 W.W. WAFFLES^
F	t	mixed fruit / Dream Whip
P	t	6 oz. skim milk

SNACK

W		12 oz.
V	t	6 oz. V-8 Juice, cauliflower

LUNCH

W		12 oz.
V		small tossed salad
G	t	baked potato with broccoli & mushrooms
F	t	apple
P	4	1 cup chili over baked potato

SNACK

W		12 oz.
G	4	2 FRUIT FILLED BRAN MUFFINS^

DINNER

W		12 oz.
V	t	SPINACH-CITRUSSALAD^
G	2	2 w.w. rolls
F		included salad
P	4	GONE ALL AFTERNOON STEW^

SNACK

W		12 oz.
G	t	grapes
P	t	1 cup nonfat lemon yogurt

TOTAL FAT GRAMS: 22

SHOPPING LIST

VEGETABLES

2 large bunches	Broccoli
2 heads	Cauliflower
2 bags	Carrots (5 lbs. ea.)
2 stalks	Celery
small container	Cherry tomatoes
1 can	Corn
4	Cucumbers
12 oz.	Fresh mushrooms
1 bunch	Fresh parsley
9 oz. pkg.	Frozen Corn
2 pkg.s	Frozen green beans (9 oz.)
2 lb. bag	Frozen hashbrowns (no fat)
2 whole	Garlic
5	Green bell peppers
1 bunch	Green onion
6 medium	Green tomatoes
2 heads	Leaf lettuce
1 head	Lettuce
1 can	Mushrooms (4 oz.)
1 can	Peas frozen (9 oz. pkg.)
1 can	Petite peas
10 lb. bag	Potatoes
1	Red bell pepper
3 small	Red onion
2 bunches	Spinach (fresh)
10 oz. pkg.	Spinach (frozen)
18 fresh	Tomatoes⎫ or 3, 28 oz. cans
28 oz. can	Tomatoes⎭
6 oz. can	Tomato paste
8 oz. can	Tomato sauce
3 cans	V-8 juice (46 oz.)
small package	Wheat sprouts
6 large	White onions
6 small	Zucchini

GRAINS

1 small box	All Bran cereal
5 lb. bag	All purpose flour
2 cans	Black beans (16 oz.)
1 bag	Brown rice
small pkg.	Bulgur wheat
1 small box	Cheerios
1 large can	Chili
1 small Box	Corn Flakes
1 dozen	Corn tortillas
1 small box	Grapenuts cereal
2 cans	Kidney beans (16 oz.)
small pkg.	Oat bran
1 small box	Oat Bran cereal
1 bag	Oatmeal
1 pkg.	Popcorn cakes
1 small loaf	Rye bread
small pkg.	Unprocessed bran
1 large box	Wheat Chex cereal
5 dozen	Whole grain rolls
2 loaves	Whole wheat bread
10 lb. bag	Whole wheat flour
small bag	Wondra flour

WEEK 1 SHOPPING LIST CONTINUED...

FRUITS

2 jars	All fruit jam
6 oz. can	Apple Cider
8 oz. jar	Applesauce
20	Bananas
12 oz. bag	Fresh or frozen whole cranberries
2	Grapefruit
1/2 cup	Grapefruit or orange juice
2 cans	Grapefruit sections
2	Green apples
2 medium	Jonathon or Granny Smith Apples
2	Kiwi
1	Lemon
3 large cans	Lite fruit cocktail
3 cans	Mandarin oranges
1 (your choice)	Melon
4	Peaches (or can in own juice)
20- oz. can	Pineapple chunks
15 1/4 oz. can	Pineapple tidbits (in own juice)
1 lb. pkg.	Raisins
1 pint cup	Raspberries
15	Red apples
2 1/2 lbs.	Red grapes
2 1/2 lbs.	Red or green grapes
3 pint cups	Strawberries

PROTEINS

DAIRY

1/2 pint	Buttermilk
3 doz.	Eggs
8 oz.	Fat free cream cheese
5 oz. pkg.	Fresh Parmesan cheese
6 oz.	Frigo Truly Lite Mozzarella Cheese
12 slice pkg.	Kraft free singles
3 oz.	Kraft Light Natural Sharp Cheese
8 oz.	Light Sour Cream
32 oz.	Low-fat cottage cheese
16 oz.	Low-fat cottage cheese
4 oz.	Low-fat plain yogurt
16 oz.	Nonfat cottage cheese
1 pint	Nonfat frozen yogurt
2 container	Nonfat lemon yogurt (32 oz.)
1 container	Nonfat lemon yogurt (4 oz.)
1 container	Nonfat plain yogurt (32 oz.)
1 container	Nonfat plain yogurt (4 oz.)
16 oz.	Nonfat Ricotta cheese
1 container	Nonfat vanilla yogurt (32 oz.)
1 container	Nonfat vanilla yogurt (8 oz.)
2 cans	Skim evaporated milk
2 1/2 gal.	Skim milk

MEATS

1 lb.	Atlantic halibut
4	Chicken breasts (5 oz.)
8	Chicken breasts (8 oz.)
2 lbs. 12 oz.	Lean top round steak
2 cans	Tuna fish (packed in water)
8 oz.	Turkey breast meat

MISCELLANEOUS

small bottle	Bechamel Sauce
small bottle	Beef bouillon
1 box	Butter Buds
1 can	Campbell's Healthy Request Cream of Mushroom soup
4 small cans	Campbell'sHealthy Request Vegetable Beef soup
1 can	Campbell's Italian Tomato soup
1 bottle	Catsup
1 bottle	Club soda (optional)
small box	Dream Whip
medium bottle	Honey
3 1/2 oz. pkg.	Instant lemon pudding mix
1	Mustard
1 bottle	Nonfat mayonnaise
small bottle	Nonfat or low-fat Italian salad dressing
1 bottle	Nonfat salad dressing (your choice)
1 box	Paper muffin cups (optional)
1 box	Pectin (used in jam)
small jar	Pickled jalapenos
1 bottle	Salsa
1 pkg.	Schillings Thick and Zesty Spaghetti Sauce mix
small pkg.	Tapioca(dry)
1 can	Tomato soup
small bottle	White wine vinegar
1 small bottle	Worcestershire sauce

BAKING

1 can	Baking powder
1 box	Baking soda
1 can	Basil
1 can	Bay leaves
1 can	Black pepper
1 lb. box	Brown sugar
1 bottle	Canola oil
1 small pkg.	Chili powder
1 can	Cinnamon
1 bottle	Coconut extract
1 can	Crushed red pepper flakes
small pkg.	Dried dill weed
1 can	Dry mustard
1 can	Dry parsley
1 lb. bag	Fructose
1 can	Ground cumin
small bottle	Lemon juice
1 can	Lemon pepper
1 can	Nutmeg
small bottle	Olive oil
1 can	Pam nonstick cooking spray
1 can	Paprika
1 small bottle	Red wine vinegar
1 box	Salt
1 bottle	Vanilla

Menus serve a family of four. **W** = Water, **V** = Veggie, **G** = Grain, **F** = Fruit, **P** = Protein

DAY 1

•	FG	BREAKFAST
W		12 oz.
V		see snack
G	2	3/4 c Nutri-grain Almond and Raisin cereal
F	t	1/2 grapefruit
P	t	6 oz. skim milk
		SNACK
W		12 oz.
V	t	6 oz. tomato juice, carrot
		LUNCH
W		12 oz.
V	t	lettuce, tomato, peppers (sandwich)
G	2	w.w. subway roll
F	t	grapes
P	5	3 oz. turkey, 1 oz. Lite Line cheese
		SNACK
W		12 oz.
V	1	celery, green pepper sticks and PINEAPPLE-PEPPER DIP^
		DINNER
W		12 oz.
V	t	tossed salad with nonfat salad dressing
G	2	GARLIC TOAST^
F	t	BROILED PINEAPPLE ROUNDS^ over 1/4 cup nonfat vanilla yogurt
P	2	BULGAR CHEESE BAKE^
		SNACK
W		12 oz.
G	1	FRUIT FILLED BRAN MUFFIN^
P	t	6 oz. skim milk

TOTAL FAT GRAMS: 14

DAY 2

•	FG	BREAKFAST
W		12 oz.
V	t	6 oz. V-8 Juice
G	2	1 1/2 c Raisin Bran cereal
F		in cereal
P	t	6 oz. skim milk
		SNACK
W		12 oz.
V	t	celery, bell pepper
		LUNCH
W		12 oz.
V	t	tomato, lettuce, bell pepper, onion
G	2	w.w. bun
F	t	sliced apple
P	3	2 (1 1/2 oz.) slices extra lean ham
	2	1 oz. Lite Line cheese
		SNACK
W		12 oz.
G	2	3/4 cup Nutri-grain Almond & Raisin cereal
P	t	6 oz. skim milk
V	t	carrot
		DINNER
W		12 oz.
V	t	OVEN FRIES^ , REFRIGERATOR COLESLAW^
G	2	2 w.w. rolls
F	t	lite fruit cocktail
P	3	BAKED CHICKEN NUGGETS^
		SNACK
W		12 oz.
G	2	2 cups MOTHER GOOSE POPCORN^

TOTAL FAT GRAMS: 18

DAY 3

•	FG	BREAKFAST
W		12 oz.
V		see snack
G		included in cup
F	t	1/2 grapefruit
P	2	2 INDIVIDUAL BREAKFAST CUPS^

SNACK

W		12 oz.
V	t	celery sticks, 2 Tbl. SPINACH DIP^

LUNCH

W		12 oz.
V	4	2 servings TURKEY-RICE APPLE SALAD^
G	2	2 w.w. rolls
F	t	peach
P		included in salad

SNACK

W		12 oz.
V	t	cut-up vegies, 1 Tbl. SPINACH DIP^

DINNER

W		12 oz.
V	t	salad, nonfat dressing
	t	1/2 c steamed broccoli, cauliflower, carrots
G	t	1 cup SKINNY MASHED POTATOES^
F	t	strawberries with non-fat lemon yogurt
P	3	3 oz. POT ROASTED EYE-OF-ROUND^

SNACK

W		12 oz.
G	2	3/4 c Nutri-grain Almond and Raisin cereal
P	t	6 oz. skim milk

TOTAL FAT GRAMS: 13

DAY 4

•	FG	BREAKFAST
W		12 oz.
V		see snack
G	2	2 FRENCH TOAST^
F	t	orange juice
P	t	1/4 c nonfat vanilla yogurt and all fruit jam

SNACK

W		12 oz.
V	t	green pepper sliced
G	10	2 w.w. toast with 2 tsp. butter

LUNCH

W		12 oz.
V	t	3/4 cup broccoli steamed
	2	baked potato with 1/2 cup low-fat cottage cheese
G	1	w.w. roll
F	t	1/2 cup applesauce
P	2	2 oz. BBQ chicken breast (microwave)

SNACK

W		12 oz.
V	t	carrot stick, pepper strips, nonfat salad dressing

DINNER

W		12 oz.
V	t	1 1/2 cups steamed spinach
G	1	w.w. roll, 1/2 cup CRUNCHY 4 GRAIN MIX^
F	t	fruit cocktail cup
P	1	SIMPLY WONDERFUL ORANGE ROUGHY^

SNACK

W		12 oz.
G	2	1 cup Cheerios
P	t	6 oz. skim milk

TOTAL FAT GRAMS: 21

DAY 5

•	FG	BREAKFAST
W		12 oz.
V		see snack
G	4	2 BANANA BREAD^
F	t	strawberries with
P	t	Pet Lite Evaporated
		Milk on top

SNACK

W		12 oz.
V	t	cut-up vegies
G	2	1 PUMPKIN MUFFIN^

LUNCH

W		12 oz.
V	t	tomato, lettuce,
		onions, peppers
G	4	2 ww. tortillas
F	t	pears
P	4	2, 1/2 c servings
		refried beans

SNACK

W		12 oz.
G	2	1 PUMPKIN MUFFIN^
V	t	1 cup frozen mixed
		vegetables with
		Molly McButter

DINNER

W		12 oz.
V	t	SPINACH-CITRUS
		SALAD^
G	1	w.w. roll
F		included in salad
P	8	TURKEY POT PIE^

SNACK

W		12 oz.
G	2	1 1/2 c Raisin Bran
F	t	banana
P	t	6 oz. skim milk

TOTAL FAT GRAMS: 27

DAY 6

•	FG	BREAKFAST
W		12 oz.
V	t	6 oz. V-8 Juice
G	1	1 1/2 cup Crispix
	1	1 slice w.w. toast with
F	t	all fruit jam
P	t	6 oz. skim milk

SNACK

W		12 oz.
F	t	orange
	5	1 w.w. toast with
		1 tsp. butter

LUNCH

W		12 oz.
V	1	baked yam with
		Butter Buds
G	1	w.w. toast, all fruit
		jam
F	t	canteloupe
P	t	6-8 oz. nonfat yogurt
		of your choice

SNACK

W		12 oz.
F	t	cut-up vegies

DINNER

W		12 oz.
V	t	salad, nonfat dressing
	t	steamed cauliflower,
		petite peas
G	4	2 GARLIC CHEESE
		TOAST^
F	t	strawberries, nonfat
		vanilla yogurt
P	6	SKILLET PASTA^

SNACK

W		12 oz.
F	1	EASY BAKED APPLES^

TOTAL FAT GRAMS: 20

DAY 7

•	FG	BREAKFAST
W		12 oz.
V		see snack
G	1	1 1/2 cup Crispex
	2	1 slice BANANA BREAD^
F	t	apple juice
P	t	6 oz. skim milk

SNACK

W		12 oz.
V	t	cucumber slices
F	t	cantelope

LUNCH

W		12 oz.
V	t	cut-up vegies & 2 Tbl. SPINACH DIP^
G	2	1 slice BANANA BREAD^
F	t	"Pam" fried pineapple
P	2	2 (1 oz.) slices pan fried extra lean ham

SNACK

W		12 oz.
V	t	microwaved sweet potato slices
G	2	FRUIT FILLED BRAN MUFFINS^

DINNER

W		12 oz.
V	t	steamed carrots
G	1	1 cup steamed bulgar wheat
F	t	fruit cup
P	6	2 servings SAVORY TURKEY BUNDLES^

SNACK

W		12 oz.
F	t	banana slices with
P	t	6 oz. skim milk

TOTAL FAT GRAMS: 15

VEGETABLES

1 large bunches	Broccoli
1 bag	Broccoli (frozen)
1 bag	Broccoli, cauliflower, carrot (frozen)
1 large head	Cauliflower
2 bags	Carrots (5 lbs. ea.)
2 stalks	Celery
5	Cucumbers
1 bunch	Fresh parsley
2 whole	Garlic
5	Green bell peppers
3 large bunches	Green onion
1 large head	Leaf lettuce
1 head	Lettuce
1 large bag	Mixed vegetables
1 small bag	Peas frozen
1 small bag	Petite peas
10 lb. bag	Potatoes
1 can	Pumpkin
2	Red bell pepper
1	Red onion
3 large bunches	Spinach, fresh
3	Spinach (10 oz. pkg. frozen)
4	Sweet potatoes
24 oz. can	Tomato juice
10 fresh	Tomatoes
28 oz. can	Tomatoes
2 cans	V-8 juice (46 oz.)
6 large	White onions
4	Yams

GRAINS

small bag	All purpose flour
small pkg.	Bran (unprocessed)
1 bag	Brown rice
1 bag	Bulgur wheat
1 small box	Cheerios
small box	Cornmeal
small box	Crispix cereal
small bag	Millet
1 box	Nutri-Grain Almond Raisin Cereal
small pkg.	Oat bran
1 pkg.	Popcorn
small box	Raisin Bran cereal
2 cans	Refried beans (16 oz.)
small pkg.	Vermicelli (uncooked)
1 dozen	Whole wheat buns
2 1/2 dozen	Whole grain rolls
3 loaves	Whole wheat bread
small bag	Whole wheat flour
4	Whole wheat subway rolls
1 dozen	Whole wheat tortillas
1 small bag	Wondra flour

WEEK 2 SHOPPING LIST CONTINUED...

FRUITS

1 jar	All fruit jam
46 oz. can	Apple juice
6	Apples
16 oz. jar	Applesauce
14	Bananas
1 large	Canteloupe
12 oz. bag	Fresh or frozen whole cranberries
4	Grapefruit
1 can	Grapefruit sections
2 lbs.	Grapes
1	Jonathan or Granny Smith apple
1	Lemon
1	Lime
3 large cans	Lite fruit cocktail
1 can	Mandarin oranges
4	Oranges
4	Peaches (or 1 can in own juice)
4	Pears
20- oz. can	Pineapple (crushed)
1 medium can	Pineapple (slices)
3 pint cups	Strawberries

PROTEINS

DAIRY

12 oz. pkg.	Bordens Fat Free Singles Swiss Cheese
1 lb.	Butter
2 doz.	Eggs
5 oz. pkg.	Fresh Parmesan cheese
10 oz.	Frigo Truly Lite Mozzarella Cheese
12 slice pkg.	Kraft free singles
8 oz.	Light Sour Cream
8 oz.	Lite Line cheese
16 oz.	Low-fat cottage cheese
2 containers	Low-fat plain yogurt (16 oz.)
8 oz.	Low-fat plain yogurt
2 tubs	Margarine (low-fat)
8 oz. bottle	Mayonnaise (nonfat)
16 oz.	Nonfat cottage cheese
1 container	Nonfat lemon yogurt (16 oz.)
1 container	Nonfat plain yogurt (16 oz.)
1 container	Nonfat vanilla yogurt (16 oz.)
1 container	Nonfat vanilla yogurt (8 oz.)
2 containers	Nonfat yogurt, your choice (16 oz.)
3 cans	Skim evaporated milk
2 gal.	Skim milk

MEATS

4 (2 oz.)	BBQ chicken breasts
1 1/2 lbs.	Chicken breast, boneless, skinless
3 lbs.	Eye-of-Round roast
12 oz.	Ham, extra lean
8 slices	Ham, extra lean (1 oz. each)
4 (4 oz.)	Orange roughy fillets
1 small	Turkey, cooked

MISCELLANEOUS

1	Beef or chicken bouillon
1 box	Butter Buds
11 oz. can	Campbell's Italian Tomato Soup
1 pkg.	Dry Italian salad dressing mix
1	Dry vegetable or leek soup mix
1 pkg.	Egg roll wrappers
1 bottle	Honey
small bottle	Hot pepper sauce
1 bottle	Molly McButter
1	Mrs. Dash garlic
1	Mrs. Dash Herb salt free seasoning
1 large bottle	Nonfat salad dressing (your choice)
1	Taco seasoning mix
20- oz. can	Turkey Broth (use from cooked turkey)
small pkg.	Walnuts or pecans
1 small can	Water chestnuts
small bottle	Wishbone Lite Italian Salad Dressing

BAKING

1 can	Baking powder
1 box	Baking soda
1 can	Basil
1 can	Bay leaves (whole)
1 lb. box	Brown sugar
1 small bottle	Canola oil
1 can	Celery seed
1 can	Cinnamon
1 can	Cream of Tartar
as desired	Food coloring
small bag	Fructose
1 can	Garlic powder
1 can	Ginger
small bottle	Lemon juice
small bottle	Molasses
1 can	Mustard seed
1 can	Nutmeg
1 small bottle	Olive oil
1 can	Oregano
1 large can	Pam nonstick spray
1 bottle	Parsley flakes
1 can	Pepper
1 box	Salt
1 can	Sage
1 can	Thyme
1 bottle	Vanilla
1 bottle	Vinegar
small bag	White sugar

DAY 1

•	FG	BREAKFAST
W		12 oz.
V		see snack
G	2	4 W.W. PANCAKES^
F	t	strawberries
P	t	1/4 c nonfat vanilla yogurt and all fruit jam
		SNACK
W		12 oz.
V	t	tomatoes and cucumbers in rice vinegar
G	1	w.w. bagel
		LUNCH
W		12 oz.
V	t	tossed salad, nonfat dressing
G		included in tuna
F	t	strawberries
P	6	2 CREAMED TUNA^ over 2 slices of toast
		SNACK
W		12 oz.
V	t	1 cup green beans, salsa
G	t	2 PUMPKIN CARROT MUFFINS^
		DINNER
W		12 oz.
V	t	tossed salad
G	2	2 w.w. rolls
F	t	fruit in season
P	7	QUICK FETTUCCINE WITH VEGETABLES^
		SNACK
W		12 oz.
G	2	1 FRUIT FILLED BRAN MUFFIN^
F	t	all fruit jam

TOTAL FAT GRAMS: 20

DAY 2

•	FG	BREAKFAST
W		12 oz.
V	t	6 oz. V-8 Juice
G	4	2 FRUIT FILLED MUFFINS^
F		in muffins
P	6	2 scrambled eggs, 1 yolk
		SNACK
W		12 oz.
V	2	cauliflower bits & 1 Tbl. SPINACH DIP^
		LUNCH
W		12 oz.
V	t	see protein
G	2	2 slices w.w. toast
F	t	1 cup unsweetened applesauce
P	2	1/2 cup low-fat cottage cheese & tomatoes
		SNACK
W		12 oz.
V	t	cut-up vegies
G	2	2 w.w. toast with all fruit jam
		DINNER
W		12 oz.
V	t	1 1/2 cups steamed broccoli, cauliflower, carrots
G	1	w.w. roll
F	t	honey dew melon
P	3	LEMON-LIME POACHED CHICKEN^
		SNACK
W		12 oz.
F	t	banana
G	1	2 squares Graham crackers

TOTAL FAT GRAMS: 23

MENU PLANS WEEK THREE

DAY 3

•	FG	BREAKFAST
W		12 oz.
V	t	onions, tomatoes, green peppers, mushrooms
G	2	2 slices w.w. toast
F	t	6 oz. unsweetened grape juice
P	6	3 egg (1 yolk) omelet with vegies cut-up

SNACK

W		12 oz.
V	t	cherry tomatoes, mushrooms, carrots

LUNCH

W		12 oz.
V	t	corn on the cob
G	2	2 slices w.w. bread
F	t	sliced tomato
P	2	2 oz. sliced turkey

SNACK

W		12 oz.
F	t	pineapple slice
P	2	1/2 cup low-fat cottage cheese

DINNER

W		12 oz.
V	t	1 cup steamed carrots
	t	mixed salad
G		included in tuna
F	t	watermelon
P	6	2 CREAMED TUNA^ over 2 slices toast

SNACK

W		12 oz.
G	2	1 1/2 c Cheerios cereal
P	t	6 oz. skim milk

	TOTAL FAT GRAMS: 22

DAY 4

•	FG	BREAKFAST
W		12 oz.
V		see snack
G	2	2 cups Grapenut Flakes
F	t	peaches
P	t	6 oz. skim milk

SNACK

W		12 oz.
V	t	sliced green peppers
G	1	1 slice w.w. toast with all fruit jam

LUNCH

W		12 oz.
V	t	tomatoes, cucumbers and celery cut-up
G	2	1/2 w.w. pita pocket
F	t	peaches
P	3	6 oz. imitation crab

SNACK

W		12 oz.
G	4	2 FRUIT FILLED BRAN MUFFIN^

DINNER

W		12 oz.
V	t	1 cup green beans
	1	STUFFED BAKED POTATOES^
G	1	whole grain roll
F	t	SPINACH-CITRUS SALAD^
P	6	CHICKEN CORDON BLEU^

SNACK

W		12 oz.
G	2	FRUIT FILLED BRAN MUFFIN^

	TOTAL FAT GRAMS: 22

DAY 5　　　　　　　　DAY 6

•	FG	BREAKFAST	•	FG	BREAKFAST
W		12 oz.	W		12 oz.
V		see snack	V		see snack
G	4	2 PUMPKIN CARROT MUFFINS^	G	2	2 slices w.w. toast
			F	t	1/2 grapefruit
	2	1 1/2 cups Wheat Hearts cereal	P	6	1 poached egg
F	t	banana			
P	t	6 oz. skim milk			**SNACK**
			W		12 oz.
		SNACK	V	t	cut-up vegies
W		12 oz.			
G	t	2 cups popcorn			**LUNCH**
			W		12 oz.
		LUNCH	V	t	see soup
W		12 oz.	G	4	toasted (1 oz.) Lite Line cheese on 2 slices w.w. bread
V	t	corn on the cob lettuce, salsa	F	t	banana slices
G	1	2 corn tortillas	P	2.5	2 cups LENTIL VEGETABLE SOUP^
F	t	cut-up tomatoes			
P	4.5	1/2 oz. cheddar cheese			**SNACK**
	2	2, 1/4 c servings refried beans	W		12 oz.
			V	t	cabbage wedge
		SNACK			
W		12 oz.			**DINNER**
V	2	celery, 1 Tbl. SPINACH DIP^	W		12 oz.
			V	1	1 cup baked banana squash
		DINNER			tossed salad
W		12 oz.	G	1	w.w. roll
V	t	crunchy red and green bell pepper strips	F	t	1 fruit cup cocktail
G	1	w.w. roll	P	4	3 OZ. BAKED PORK TENDERLOIN^
F	t	BROILED PINEAPPLE ROUND^			
P	2.5	2 cups LENTIL VEGETABLE SOUP^			**SNACK**
			W		12 oz.
		SNACK	G	2	1 1/2 cups Raisin Bran cereal
W		12 oz.	P	t	6 oz. skim milk
F	t	banana, grapes			
TOTAL FAT GRAMS: 18			**TOTAL FAT GRAMS: 22.5**		

DAY 7

MENU PLANS WEEK THREE

.	FG	BREAKFAST
W		12 oz.
V		see snack
G	3	3 FRENCH TOAST^
F	t	1/2 grapefruit
P		included in toast

SNACK

W		12 oz.
V	t	broccoli & celery, 2 Tbl.
		LOW-FAT VEGIE DIP^

LUNCH

W		12 oz.
V	t	tomato, lettuce
G	2	2 w.w. bread
F	t	apple
P	6	2 oz. turkey breast

SNACK

| W | | 12 oz. |
| V | t | baby carrots |

DINNER

W		12 oz.
V		included in stir fry
G	t	1/2 cup STEAMED
		BROWN RICE^
	1	w.w. roll
F	t	pineapple slices
P	1	1 serving TERRIFIC
		TURKEY STIR-FRY^

SNACK

W		12 oz.
G	2	1cup serving oatmeal
		cereal
P	t	6 oz. skim milk

TOTAL FAT GRAMS: 15

VEGETABLES

1 bag	Baby carrots
1 medium	Banana squash
1 large bunch	Broccoli
2 bag	Broccoli, cauliflower, carrot (frozen)
1 small head	Cabbage
1 large head	Cauliflower
1 bag	Carrots (5 lbs. ea.)
2 stalks	Celery
1 small basket	Cherry tomatoes
8	Corn on the Cob
6	Cucumbers
2 bunches	Fresh parsley
3	Green bell peppers
4 cans	Green beans
2 bunches	Green onion
2 heads	Lettuce
3 lbs.	Mushrooms, fresh
5 lb. bag	Potatoes
16 oz. can	Pumpkin
3	Red bell pepper
1	Red onion
7	White onions
1 large bunch	Spinach
10 oz. pkg.	Spinach, frozen chopped
11	Tomatoes
46 oz. can	V-8 Juice

GRAIN

5 lb. bag	All purpose flour
1 small bag	Brown rice
small box	Cheerios
1 dozen	Corn tortillas
small bag	Dry Lentils
8 oz.	Fettucini
1 small box	Graham Crackers
1 box	Grapenuts Flakes
small bag	Oat bran
small bag	Oatmeal (regular)
2 lbs.	Popcorn
small box	Raisin Bran cereal
16 oz. can	Refried beans
small pkg.	Seasoned dried bread crumbs
small bag	Unprocessed bran
1 box	Wheat Hearts
1 loaf	Whole grain bread
small bag	Whole grain flour
4	Whole grain rolls
4	Whole wheat bagel
5 loaves	Whole wheat bread
5 lb. bag	Whole wheat flour
1 pkg.	Whole wheat pita pockets
2 dozen	Whole wheat rolls
small bag	Wondra flour

WEEK 3 SHOPPING LIST CONTINUED...

FRUIT

1 jar	All fruit jam
4	Apples
32 oz. jar	Applesauce, unsweetened
2	Apples, Jonathan
12	Bananas
1 bag	Cranberries, fresh or frozen
1	Fresh line
4	Fruit in season, own choice
4	Grapefruit
1 can	Grapefruit sections
3 cans	Grape juice, frozen unsweetened (12 oz.)
1	Honey dew melon
1 large can	Lite fruit cocktail
1 can	Mandarin oranges
1 lb. bag	Raisins
8	Peaches
3 cans	Pineapple slices (in own juice)
2 pint cups	Strawberries
1 small	Watermelon

PROTEIN

DAIRY

2 oz.	Cheddar cheese
8 oz.	Fat free cream cheese
5 oz. pkg.	Fresh parmesan cheese
1/2 oz.	Frigo Truly Lite Mozzarella cheese
3 dozen	Eggs
3 oz.	Kraft Light Naturals Swiss cheese
8 oz.	Light sour cream
4 oz.	Lite Line cheese
3 (16 oz.)	Low-fat cottage cheese
8 oz.	Nonfat cottage cheese
16 oz.	Nonfat cottage cheese
32 oz. container	Nonfat plain yogurt
3 oz.	Nonfat vanilla yogurt
2 cans	Skim evaporated milk
1 gal.	Skim milk

MEATS

8 (4 oz.)	Chicken breasts (boneless, skinless
12 oz.	Chicken , boneless, skinless
10 oz.	Ham, extra lean
24 oz.	Imitation crab
1 lb.	Pork Tenderloin
6 cans (6 oz.)	Tuna fish (packed in water)
1 lb.	Turkey breast meat
8 oz.	Turkey, sliced

MISCELLANEOUS

1 box	Butter Buds
1 can	Campbell's Healthy Request Low-fat Cream of Chicken Soup
small bottle	Catsup
small bottle	Club soda
4 cans	Condensed chicken broth (low sodium)) 10 3/4 oz.
1 jar	Dijon Mustard
1 pkg.	Dry Italian salad dressing mix
1 pkg.	Dry vegetable or leek soup mix
	Ham Broth (use recipe or you can substitute it with 4 (14 1/2 oz.) canned chicken broth (low sodium)
1 bottle	Honey
1 bottle	Kraft nonfat mayonnaise
1 bottle	Nonfat salad dressing (your choice)
1 box	Pectin
1 bottle	Salsa
small bottle	Stir fry sauce
2 small cans	Water chestnuts
small bottle	Worcestershire sauce

BAKING

1 can	Baking powder
1 box	Baking soda
1 can	Basil
1 bag	Brown sugar
small bottle	Canola oil
1 bottle	Chicken bouillon granules
1 can	Cinnamon
1 box	Cornstarch
small bag	Fructose
1 can	Leaf tarragon
1 bottle	Lemon juice
1 can	Marjoram leaves
1 can	Nutmeg
1 can	Onion powder
1 can	Paprika
1 can	Pepper
1 can	Poppy seeds
1 small bottle	Rice vinegar
1 box	Salt
1 bottle	Vanilla

Menus serve a family of four. **W** = Water, **V** = Veggie, **G** = Grain, **F** = Fruit, **P** = Protein

DAY 1

•	FG	BREAKFAST
W		12 oz.
V		see snack
G	2	2 w.w. toast
F	t	banana
P	t	1 cup nonfat lemon yogurt and 1/2 cup fruit cocktail

SNACK

W		12 oz.
V	t	green pepper & LOW-FAT VEGIE DIP^

LUNCH

W		12 oz.
V	t	baby carrots
G	2	2 w.w. bread
F	t	grapes
P	2	1 oz. slice grilled Lite Line cheese sandwich
	1	1 oz. extra lean ham

SNACK

W		12 oz.
V	t	cut-up vegies and LOW-FAT VEGIE DIP^
G	4	2 ICE BOX BRAN MUFFINS^

DINNER

W		12 oz.
V	t	salad, nonfat dressing
G	2	2 w.w. rolls
F	t	SPINACH-CITRUS SALAD^
P	1	1 serving QUICK VEGETABLE & TWO BEAN CHILI^ Top with:
	2	2 Tbl. cheddar cheese, 1Tbl. lite sour cream & onions

SNACK

W		12 oz.
F	t	banana

DAY 2

•	FG	BREAKFAST
W		12 oz.
V		see snack
G	2	1 cup serving Oatmeal
F	t	1/2 cup raisins
P	t	6 oz. skim milk

SNACK

W		12 oz.
V	t	celery sticks

LUNCH

W		12 oz.
V	t	carrot sticks
G	t	microwaved potato
F	t	sliced apples
P	1	1 serving VEGETABLE AND 2 BEAN CHILI^
	2	2 Tbl. cheddar cheese

SNACK

W		12 oz.
G	2	1 ICE BOX BRAN MUFFIN^

DINNER

W		12 oz.
V	t	petite peas
G	1	1 cup STEAMED BROWN RICE^
F	t	pinapple chunks
P	6	1 cup STICKY CHICKEN^

SNACK

W		12 oz.
G	6	1 cup Raisin Nut Bran cereal
P	t	6 oz. skim milk

TOTAL FAT GRAMS: 16	TOTAL FAT GRAMS: 20

DAY 3

•	FG	BREAKFAST
W		12 oz.
V		see snack
G	t	1 c CRACKED WHEAT CEREAL^ (honey)
F	t	1 banana, 1/4 c raisins
P	t	1 c skim milk

SNACK

W		12 oz.
G	t	6 oz. nonfat yogurt (your choice) with Grapenuts added
	2	1 ICE BOX BRAN MUFFINS^

LUNCH

W		12 oz.
V	t	salad with nonfat dressing
G	2	2 slices w.w. toast
F	t	sliced apple
P	2	8 oz. chicken noodle soup

SNACK

W		12 oz.
V	t	cut-up vegies
F	t	sliced apples

DINNER

W		12 oz.
V	t	steamed carrots and celery sticks
G	2	2 whole grain roll
F	t	canteloupe
P	3	PIZZA STYLE SPAGHETTI^

SNACK

W		12 oz.
G	4	2 ICE BOX BRAN MUFFINS^
F	t	all fruit jam

TOTAL FAT GRAMS: 15

DAY 4

•	FG	BREAKFAST
W		12 oz.
V		see snack
G	t	2 w.w. toast
F	t	all fruit jam,
	t	1/2 grapefruit
P	6	1 fried egg in butter-flavored Pam

SNACK

W		12 oz.
V	t	2 c popcorn with Butter Buds

LUNCH

W		12 oz.
V	t	tomato, lettuce, onions, peppers
G	4	2 ww. tortillas
F	t	pears
P	4	2 servings (1/2 cup each) refried beans
	2	2 Tbl. cheddar cheese

SNACK

W		12 oz.
V	t	cut-up vegies and LOW-FAT VEGGIE DIP^

DINNER

W		12 oz.
V	t	1/2 cup green beans
	t	tossed salad
G	1	1 w.w. bread
F	t	sliced tomatoes
P	4	YUMMY LAYERED CASSEROLE^

SNACK

W		12 oz.
G	2	2 w.w. toast
F	t	all fruit jam

TOTAL FAT GRAMS: 23

DAY 5

•	FG	BREAKFAST
W		12 oz.
V	t	8 oz. V-8 Juice
G	1	1 w.w. toast with
F	t	all fruit jam
P	t	1/2 c nonfat vanilla yogurt with fruit cocktail
		SNACK
W		12 oz.
V	t	jicama slices
G	2	ICE BOX BRAN MUFFIN^
		LUNCH
W		12 oz.
V	4	steamed broccoli, cauliflower & carrots with 2 (1 oz.) slices melted Lite Line cheese
G	2	2 w.w. toast
F	t	1 large orange
P	t	1 cup skim milk
		SNACK
W		12 oz.
G	1	1 cup Wheaties cereal
F	t	raisins
P	t	1 cup skim milk
		DINNER
W		12 oz.
V	t	salad with nonfat dressing, petite peas
G	2	2 w.w. toast
F	t	FRESH FRUIT WITH LEMONY DIPPING SAUCE^
P	4	2 servings BARBEQUE TURKEY^ over 1 cup
	1	STEAMED BROWN RICE^
		SNACK
W		12 oz.
F	t	1 slice cantaloupe
G	2	1 ICE BOX BRAN MUFFIN^

TOTAL FAT GRAMS: 19

DAY 6

•	FG	BREAKFAST
W		12 oz.
V		see snack
G	3	3 FRENCH TOAST^
F	t	1/2 cantaloupe
P	t	1/2 cup nonfat vanilla yogurt
		SNACK
W		12 oz.
V	t	cut-up vegies
F	t	sliced apple
		LUNCH
W		12 oz.
V	t	salad
G	2	2 slices w.w. bread
F	1	banana
P	t	1/2 cup nonfat vanilla yogurt
	2	2 oz. turkey breast
		SNACK
W		12 oz.
V	t	2 stalks celery with LOW-FAT DIP^
G	t	2 cups popcorn with Butter Buds
		DINNER
W		12 oz.
V	t	steamed spinach
G	1	1 cup BROWN RICE PILAF^
	6	2 w.w. roll with 1 tsp. butter each and all fruit jam
F	t	lite syrup peaches
P	3	MICRO-BAKED FISH^
		SNACK
W		12 oz.
G	1	1 cup Wheaties cereal
P	t	1 cup skim milk

TOTAL FAT GRAMS: 19

DAY 7

·	FG	BREAKFAST
W		12 oz.
V		see snack
G	8	2 W.W. WAFFLES^
F	t	1/2 grapefruit
P	t	1/2 cup vanilla nonfat yogurt and all fruit jam

SNACK

·		
W		12 oz.
V	t	cauliflower, carrots
G	2	1 ICE BOX BRAN MUFFIN^

LUNCH

·		
W		12 oz.
V	t	lettuce, nonfat mayo
G	2	2 slices w.w. bread
F	t	tomato
P	3	2 (1 1/2 oz.) slices extra lean ham
	2	1 oz. slice Lite Line cheese

SNACK

·		
W		12 oz.
V	t	cut-up vegies with LOW-FAT VEGIE DIP^

DINNER

·		
W		12 oz.
V	t	green beans
G	2	2 w.w. rolls
F	t	sliced apples, oranges, bananas salad
P	4	BRANDON'S BEEF NOODLE STROGANOFF^

SNACK

·		
W		12 oz.
F	t	bananas
P	t	6 oz. skim milk

TOTAL FAT GRAMS: 23

SHOPPING LIST

VEGETABLES

1 bag	Baby carrots
2 bunches	Broccoli
1 large bag	Broccoli, cauliflower, carrot (frozen)
2 heads	Cauliflower
2 bags	Carrots (5 lbs. ea.)
2 stalks	Celery
5	Cucumbers
1 large whole	Garlic
3	Green bell peppers
4 cans	Green beans
2	Jicama
1 bunch	Leaf lettuce
2 heads	Lettuce
2 (8 oz.)	Mushrooms, fresh
small bunch	Parsley
1 bag	Petite peas
5 lb. bag	Potatoes
1	Red onion
6	White onions
2 large bunches	Spinach
7	Tomatoes
2 (35 oz.)	Tomatoes canned
4	Tomato sauce (8 oz. can)
46 oz. can	V-8 Juice
3 small	Zucchini

GRAIN

small box	All Bran cereal
5 lb. bag	All purpose flour
4 cans	Black beans (16 oz.)
small pkg.	Bran buds
1 small bag	Brown rice
small bag	Bulgur wheat
small bag	Dry bread crumbs
1 box	Grapenuts
small bag	Oatmeal (regular)
2 lbs.	Popcorn
small box	Raisin Nut Bran cereal
2 cans	Refried beans (16 oz.)
2 pkg.s	Rotelle macaroni (12 oz.)
1 pkg.	Spaghetti noodles
small bag	Unground wheat kernels
2 loaves	Whole grain bread
1 dozen	Whole grain rolls
small box	Wheaties
5 loaves	Whole wheat bread
5 lb. bag	Whole wheat flour
1 pkg.	Whole wheat tortillas
2 dozen	Whole wheat rolls

WEEK 4 SHOPPING LIST CONTINUED...

FRUIT

1 jar	Apricot all fruit jam
1 jar	All fruit jam (your choice)
12	Apples
23	Bananas
3	Cantaloupe
4	Grapefruit
1 can	Grapefruit sections
2 lbs.	Grape
1	Lemon
2 cans	Lite fruit cocktail
2 cans	Mandarin oranges
6	Oranges
1 can	Orange juice, frozen
2 lb. bag	Raisins
2	Peaches
1 can	Peaches in lite syrup
2	Pears
2 cans	Pineapple chunks (in own juice)
1 can	Pineapple tidbits (optional)

PROTEIN

DAIRY

1 lb.	Butter
2 lb. brick	Cheddar cheese
8 oz.	Fat free cream cheese
5 oz. pkg.	Fresh parmesan cheese
5 oz.	Frigo Truly Lite Mozzarella cheese
2 1/2 dozen	Eggs
8 oz.	Light sour cream
8 oz.	Light sour cream and onions
16 oz.	Lite Line cheese
1 quart	Low-fat buttermilk
2 (16 oz.)	Low-fat cottage cheese
8 oz.	Nonfat lemon yogurt
2 (16 oz.)	Nonfat lemon yogurt
16 oz.	Nonfat plain yogurt
2 (32 oz.)	Nonfat vanilla yogurt
24 oz.	Nonfat yogurt (your choice)
2 gal.	Skim milk

MEATS

12 oz.	Beef top round steak, lean
2 lbs.	Chicken breasts (boneless, skinless)
1/2 lb.	Ground beef (95% fat free)
18 oz.	Ham, extra lean
1 lb.	Halibut fillets
1 lb.	Turkey breast, boneless, skinless

MISCELLANEOUS

16 oz.	Beef broth (or substitute with beef bouillon)
1 box	Butter Buds
1 can	Campbell's Italian Tomato soup
1 bottle	Catalina salad dressing, nonfat
small bottle	Catsup
2 cans	Chicken Noodle Soup
1 can	Condensed Consomme, undiluted
1 jar	Dijon Mustard
1 can	French onion soup
1 jar	Healthy Choice Spaghetti sauce (28 oz.)
1 pkg.	Hidden Valley Ranch Dressing Mix
1 bottle	Honey
small bottle	Hot pepper sauce
1 pkg.	Lipton Dry Onion Soup Mix
1 bottle	Mayonnaise, nonfat
1 bottle	Nonfat salad dressing (your choice)
1 bottle	Red wine vinegar
1 bkg.	Pectin (used in jam)
1 bottle	Worcestershire sauce

BAKING

1 can	Baking powder
1 box	Baking soda
1 can	Basil
1 can	Bay leaves
small bottle	Canola oil
1 can	Cayenne pepper
small bag	Chili powder
1 box	Cornstarch
1 can	Dry mustard
small bag	Fructose
1 can	Garlic powder
1 can	Ground Cumin
1 bottle	Lemon juice
1 can	Oregano
1 can	Pam, butter flavored
1 can	Paprika
1 bottle	Parsley flakes
1 can	Pepper
1 can	Poppy seeds
1 box	Salt
1 can	Thyme

INGREDIENT INDEX

INGREDIENT INDEX

INGREDIENT INDEX

INGREDIENT INDEX

INGREDIENT
INDEX

INGREDIENT
INDEX

INGREDIENT
INDEX

RECIPE INDEX

RECIPE INDEX

173

RECIPE
INDEX

PRODUCTS

EAT & Be Lean™ Manual
By THORNOCK INTERNATIONAL PRODUCTIONS, INC.

The Eat & Be Lean book is a practical and easy to understand manual for learning the principles needed to obtain optimum health and leanness. This is a program that the entire family will benefit from regardless of age, or condition. The principles are the same whether overweight, underweight or just the right weight, young or old. Learn why diets only make you fatter. Understand the importance of eating to complete satisfaction on the proper balance of foods, three to six times per day. You will receive 2 months of menu plans, quick recipes and shopping lists that make it easy for you to implement the program into your regular daily routine. Discover the power of the "Three Part Formula for Success" that greatly speeds your progress towards permanent leanness and allows you to get on with the rest of your life. Learn why sweets are not forbidden when eaten after a meal. Enjoy the forgiving nature of your body when you splurge.

AEROBIC-TIPS Aerobics Video
By THORNOCK INTERNATIONAL PRODUCTIONS, INC.

Aerobic-TIPS is a one hour low-impact aerobics video that opens a whole new approach to aerobic dance. It is designed specifically for the *EAT & Be Lean* program and is a unique, enjoyable and efficient way to burn fat. It offers a triple bonus to participants. One, it has two complete programs of 30 and 60 minutes that are great for all ages. Two, throughout the exercise routines, the EAT & Be Lean principles and sound exercise techniques are constantly being reinforced. Three, positive subliminal messages are continuously reinforcing the same principles and encouraging you while you exercise. Participants are all family members ranging in age from 11 to 88.

PRODUCTS

AEROBIKIDS Aerobics Video
By THORNOCK INTERNATIONAL PRODUCTIONS, INC.

Aerobikids is a low-impact video that is being used in elementary school fitness programs throughout the United States and Canada as well as by individuals in their own homes. The aerobics are safe, fun and great for kids and adults. The tape contains a 15 and 25 minute program including a pre-warm up, stretch out, pre-cardio, aerobic workout, walking cool down, and final flexibility . Simplified diet information on the subjects of anorexia, bulimia and nutrition principles adds the finishing touch.

EAT & Be Lean ™
AUDIO CASSETTE COURSE
By THORNOCK INTERNATIONAL PRODUCTIONS, INC.

The nine week audio course is taught in an actual classroom setting. It creates the same charisma and excitement you would feel and be a part of in a live session. The album has eight audio cassette tapes (one hour each), that provide the nine class sessions. The tapes feature testimonials from many Eat & Be Lean students who have achieved great health and freedom from diets and excess fat. Repetition increases the retention of these sound truths. By listening to each lesson over and over, you tune out that nagging voice in your head that keeps whispering, "You know you can't eat to be lean." The tapes make a great addition to your home library. They answer many questions that the manual alone cannot begin to cover.

WALKING WORKOUT
By THORNOCK INTERNATIONAL PRODUCTIONS, INC.

This one hour audio cassette program is filled with fun, motivating music and subliminal messages that continually reinforce the same principles taught in the classes. Positive messages such as "Success is a way of life for me" and "I am a naturally lean person", encourage a happier, healthier, leaner you. The Walking Workout has a warm-up pace, a faster training pace and a cool down pace that encourages a fun, safe workout. It is also great walking music. Since the music matches the Aerobic-TIPS video music selections, you will be able to conveniently take the Walking Workout audio cassette tape with you on vacations and perform the aerobics program you've learned through the video tape.

EAT & Be Lean™ Success Story Audio
Cassettes Tape #1 or #2
By THORNOCK INTERNATIONAL PRODUCTIONS, INC.

Eat & Be Lean realizes your need for encouraging words from others who have proven the program to be successful in their own lives. There may be many experiences similar to your own that you will be able to relate to.

Each audio cassette contains several personal stories of people who call in voluntarily to express their appreciation for the wonderful changes that are taking place in their lives and the lives of their families. They share their successes without solicitation because they are interested in helping others find the same happiness they are experiencing.

These motivating stories will touch your heart as you get to know the individuals sharing them.

Set For Life - Recipe Book
By Jane Merrill and Karen Sunderland

Now in its fourth printing, newly revised and enlarged *Set For Life* features more than 350 tasty low-fat, low sugar recipes that help you make the life-style changes you desire. These delicious family favorites are easy and fast to prepare. In addition, *Set For Life* combines the positive, highly motivating, easy-to-read style of its authors with the latest research on body fat control. Order your copy of this best-seller and do what its pages outline.

The Complete and Up-To-Date FAT Book
By Karen J. Bellerson

The *Fat Book* is an excellent resource book to be used in combination with the *EAT & Be Lean* ™ manual. The *EAT & Be Lean* manual supplies you with nutritional facts on over 700 commonly eaten foods. The *Fat Book* expands that to over 15,000 foods with complete fat and calorie information. Totaling your caloric intake once per month allows you to make certain you are eating plenty of high quality calories. It helps to adjust your fat gain intake to within 10 to 20 percent of your gradually increasing caloric intake. The *Fat Book* is an inexpensive, highly valuable tool in your quest towards permanent leanness and excellent health. It is small enough to carry in your purse or brief case.

The Quest For Love and Self-Esteem
By Virginia Bourgeous

Virginia provides an understanding of the keys necessary for quality inter-personal relationships. She shows you ways to gain love and self-esteem. She explains how to deal with perfectionists know-it-alls, dictators, martyrs, nomads, hypochondriacs and loners. Virginia discusses why people feel unloved. Man's basic needs are identified and the author explains the methods used to satisfy emotional needs.

Two chapters on parent-child relations explain how to achieve fulfillment in the parental roll, while discussing the special problems of teen-agers.

The relationship of depression to self-esteem is the timeless subject of the final chapter, discussing major causes of depression. Excellent suggestions are given concerning the overcoming of such problems.

The Quest For Love and Self-Esteem is a book that can help you help yourself. Its subject is universal and its counsel is sound.

The Support Group Packet
By THORNOCK INTERNATIONAL PRODUCTIONS, INC.

For the cost of the materials and shipping only, you can receive the information you need to begin a support group in your area. The packet contains general information about setting up the support group, a group registration form, a class roll, a personal contract master for copying, distributor information, demonstration ideas for each lesson and an enrollment application for the group members to join the Cruising Club.

Many support groups are forming all over the world as people come together to learn and share new information about this wonderful way of life.

Introductory Seminar Videos
EAT & Be Lean™ in a Nutshell
By THORNOCK INTERNATIONAL PRODUCTIONS, INC.

The EAT & Be Lean program is presented in a one hour seminar. Learn why the body becomes an efficient fat burning machine. The program provides a basic understanding of fats, sweets, calories, artificial sweeteners, muscle, exercise, positive thinking, high energy and low energy foods, and much more. Learn why diets do not create a healthy lean body. Discover the three part formula for success and understand how to apply its principles.

This video is a wonderful way to introduce the program to family and friends. It also serves as continuous motivation as you learn to implement the concepts taught through the EAT & Be Lean program.

PRODUCTS

QTY.	PRODUCT	PRICE	TOTAL
	EAT & Be Lean Favorite Family Recipes	$ 16.95	
	EAT & Be Lean Book (Student Manual)	$ 19.95	
	9 WEEK AUDIO COURSE - (No Manual)	$ 69.95	
	AEROBIC-TIPS VIDEO	$ 29.95	
	AEROBIKIDS VIDEO	$ 24.95	
	WALKING WORKOUT	$ 12.95	
	SUCCESS STORIES AUDIOS 1 OR 2	$ 9.95 each	
	FAT COUNTER BOOK	$ 6.00	
	SET FOR LIFE BOOK	$ 16.95	
	QUEST FOR LOVE & SELF ESTEEM	$ 6.95	
	SUPPORT GROUP PACKET	$ 4.00	

MAIL TO: THORNOCK INTERNATIONAL PRODUCTIONS, INC.
P.O. Box 1132
Clearfield, UT 84015

PHONE ORDERS CALL:
801-776-1176

Prices subject to change without notice

SUBTOTAL	
Utah residents add 6.25% sales tax	
TOTAL	

Name_____

Phone _____Address_____

City_____State_____Zip_____

Charge Card # _____

Card: ☐ Master Card ☐ Visa   Expiration Date _____

QTY.	PRODUCT	PRICE	TOTAL
	EAT & Be Lean Favorite Family Recipes	$ 16.95	
	EAT & Be Lean Book (Student Manual)	$ 19.95	
	9 WEEK AUDIO COURSE - (No Manual)	$ 69.95	
	AEROBIC-TIPS VIDEO	$ 29.95	
	AEROBIKIDS VIDEO	$ 24.95	
	WALKING WORKOUT	$ 12.95	
	SUCCESS STORIES AUDIOS 1 OR 2	$ 9.95 each	
	FAT COUNTER BOOK	$ 6.00	
	SET FOR LIFE BOOK	$ 16.95	
	QUEST FOR LOVE & SELF ESTEEM	$ 6.95	
	SUPPORT GROUP PACKET	$ 4.00	

MAIL TO: THORNOCK INTERNATIONAL PRODUCTIONS, INC.
P.O. Box 1132
Clearfield, UT 84015

PHONE ORDERS CALL:
801-776-1176

Prices subject to change without notice

SUBTOTAL	
Utah residents add 6.25% sales tax	
TOTAL	

Name_____

Phone _____Address_____

City_____State_____Zip_____

Charge Card # _____

Card: ☐ Master Card ☐ Visa   Expiration Date _____

QTY.	PRODUCT	PRICE	TOTAL
	EAT & Be Lean Favorite Family Recipes	$ 16.95	
	EAT & Be Lean Book (Student Manual)	$ 19.95	
	9 WEEK AUDIO COURSE - (No Manual)	$ 69.95	
	AEROBIC-TIPS VIDEO	$ 29.95	
	AEROBIKIDS VIDEO	$ 24.95	
	WALKING WORKOUT	$ 12.95	
	SUCCESS STORIES AUDIOS 1 OR 2	$ 9.95 each	
	FAT COUNTER BOOK	$ 6.00	
	SET FOR LIFE BOOK	$ 16.95	
	QUEST FOR LOVE & SELF ESTEEM	$ 6.95	
	SUPPORT GROUP PACKET	$ 4.00	

MAIL TO: THORNOCK INTERNATIONAL PRODUCTIONS, INC.
P.O. Box 1132
Clearfield, UT 84015

PHONE ORDERS CALL:
801-776-1176

Prices subject to change without notice

SUBTOTAL	
Utah residents add 6.25% sales tax	
TOTAL	

Name_____

Phone _____Address_____

City_____State_____Zip_____

Charge Card # _____

Card: ☐ Master Card ☐ Visa   Expiration Date _____

- -

QTY.	PRODUCT	PRICE	TOTAL
	EAT & Be Lean Favorite Family Recipes	$ 16.95	
	EAT & Be Lean Book (Student Manual)	$ 19.95	
	9 WEEK AUDIO COURSE - (No Manual)	$ 69.95	
	AEROBIC-TIPS VIDEO	$ 29.95	
	AEROBIKIDS VIDEO	$ 24.95	
	WALKING WORKOUT	$ 12.95	
	SUCCESS STORIES AUDIOS 1 OR 2	$ 9.95 each	
	FAT COUNTER BOOK	$ 6.00	
	SET FOR LIFE BOOK	$ 16.95	
	QUEST FOR LOVE & SELF ESTEEM	$ 6.95	
	SUPPORT GROUP PACKET	$ 4.00	

MAIL TO: THORNOCK INTERNATIONAL PRODUCTIONS, INC.
P.O. Box 1132
Clearfield, UT 84015

PHONE ORDERS CALL:
801-776-1176

Prices subject to change without notice

SUBTOTAL	
Utah residents add 6.25% sales tax	
TOTAL	

Name_____

Phone _____Address_____

City_____State_____Zip_____

Charge Card # _____

Card: ☐ Master Card ☐ Visa   Expiration Date _____

PRODUCTS

FAVORITE PERSONAL RECIPES

FAVORITE PERSONAL RECIPES

FAVORITE PERSONAL RECIPES

FAVORITE PERSONAL RECIPES

FAVORITE PERSONAL RECIPES

FAVORITE PERSONAL RECIPES

FAVORITE PERSONAL RECIPES